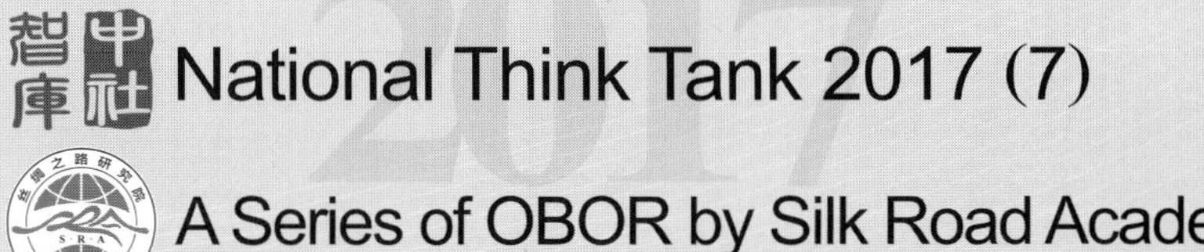

Expanding the Belt and Road : A New Perspective on China – Latin America Integrated Cooperation

Institute of Latin American Studies (ILAS),
Chinese Academy of Social Sciences (CASS)
Translated by Jia Wenyuan, Liang Xiang, et al.

中国社会科学出版社
CHINA SOCIAL SCIENCES PRESS

图书在版编目（CIP）数据

“一带一路”合作空间拓展：中拉整体合作新视角 = Expanding the Belt and Road : A New Perspective on China—Latin America Integrated Cooperation : 英文 / 中国社会科学院拉丁美洲研究所著. —北京：中国社会科学出版社，2017.5（2017.7重印）

（国家智库报告）

ISBN 978 – 7 – 5203 – 0383 – 5

Ⅰ.①一…　Ⅱ.①中…　Ⅲ.①“一带一路”—国际合作—研究—中国、拉丁美洲—英文　Ⅳ.①F125.573

中国版本图书馆 CIP 数据核字（2017）第 086495 号

出 版 人　赵剑英
责任编辑　喻　苗　侯苗苗
责任校对　韩天炜
责任印制　李寡寡

出　　版　中国社会科学出版社
社　　址　北京鼓楼西大街甲 158 号
邮　　编　100720
网　　址　http://www.csspw.cn
发 行 部　010 – 84083685
门 市 部　010 – 84029450
经　　销　新华书店及其他书店

印刷装订　北京君升印刷有限公司
版　　次　2017 年 5 月第 1 版
印　　次　2017 年 7 月第 2 次印刷

开　　本　710 × 1000　1/16
印　　张　12.5
字　　数　140 千字
定　　价　78.00 元

Preface

From both what happened in the United States and Europe and what the political economy perspective of the world would expect, anyone may predict a weakening trend of the economic globalization in at least the near future. That is, the predictable politics and economic policies in the western countries, which have been the major drivers of the previous wave of globalization, tend to drive down the economic globalization, alongside nationalism and populism dominate the policy-making of international trade and investment flows in a quite few countries.

That trend does not necessarily mean a catastrophe for China's economic growth, though it has benefited from the previous economic globalization. China will accomplish its goals of building a moderately prosperous society in all respects in 2020 and realizing its great rejuvenation in 2050, no matter what happens to the globalization. China, however, does hope that there will be a sound environment of international trade, capital flows, mobility of the talented, and other factors that economic globalization can bring in.

As the beneficiary of the globalization, the second largest economy, a country trading the largest volume of commodities internationally, and other number ones, China is indeed willing to initiate and lead the potentially next wave of economic globalization. In addition, China is also obligated to seek a change in global system of governance on behave of its own, other developing countries, and other emerging markets. All those can help developing countries in general and emerging markets in particular to gain bigger say in global governance and bigger share of globalization dividends.

The Silk Road Economic Belt and 21st Century Maritime Silk Road Initiative proposed by Chinese President Xi Jinping, taking ancient land and maritime silk road as a symbol, aims to develop economic collaboration relationships and partnerships with countries along the belt and road, build a community with political mutual trust, economic integration and cultural inclusion. This initiative covers the core of economic globalization, seeks to construct new global governance framework, and is expected to become the tipping point of next wave of economic globalization. It aims to link the Chinese domestic development to the world development, to push forward the collaboration of real economy and production capacity among countries, and to extend domestic pattern of transferring manufacturing from coastal to inland regions to international "flying geese paradigm".

Before the global system of governance fully changes to more represent interests of developing countries, the Belt and Road Initiative and its corresponding institutional arrangements, such as Asian Infrastructure Investment Bank can supplement the defects of the existing system. On the other hand, one should not forget that the Belt and Road Initiative's original purpose, that is, serving to fill the worldwide financial gap in constructing infrastructure.

Since the Belt and Road Initiative was proposed in 2013, over 100 countries and international organizations have responded positively, and 40 of them have signed cooperative agreements with China. Chinese enterprises' investments in countries along the belt and road amount to more than 50 billion US dollars, which serves to facilitate a host of major projects, boom economic development and expand employment in host countries. As President Xi put it, while the Belt and Road Initiative comes from China, it benefits the world.

In front of readers is a series of books, on the theme of the Belt and Road Initiative and its practices in various localities. Those books include (1) A Field Investigation Report on the 21st Century Maritime Silk Road; (2) The Alignment of the Silk Road Economic Belt and the Bright Road of Kazakhstan: Problems and Perspective; (3) The International Risk and Cooperative Space Expansion of the Belt and Road Initiative—the Example of Sri Lanka; (4) Port and Port Cities in Building of the Belt and Road; (5) Study on "21st Century Maritime Silk Road" Docking with "Global Maritime Fulcrum": Research Report about Fujian Province of China and Indonesia; (6) Expanding the Belt and Road : A New Perspective on China—Latin America Integrated Cooperation; (7) The Construction and Development of Asia and Africa Economic Circle under the Belt and Road Perspective; (8) The Development in the Four Economic Corridors of Indian Ocean under the Chinese Belt and Road Perspective. I hope readers, both theorists and practitioners, will find them helpful.

Cai Fang

Vice President of the Chinese Academy of Social Science

Beijing, May 4, 2017

Contents

General Report

Expansion of Cooperation Scope on "the Belt and Road Initiative": A Research on Status Quo, Opportunities and Challenges of Sino – Latin American Integrated Cooperation

Zhang Yong and Shi Peiran

Abstract: In accordance with the spirit of CCP Eighteenth Congress and the "Thirteenth Five – Year Planning" framework, China will further advance her practice with Reform and Opening up Policy, and will continue to implement the "Going Global" strategy. China has proposed the initiative to jointly develop "Silk Road Economy Belt" and "21st Century Maritime Silk Road" (hereinafter referred to as "the Belt and Road"). This is an important measure for mutually promoting opening up internally and externally, better integrating attracting foreign investment and going global, and accelerating the cultivation of the new advantages in participating and leading international economic coopetition.

Latin America and the Caribbean area (hereinafter referred to as "Latin America") as a developing region with vast territory and large population, are the important fulcrums for the implementation of China's comprehensive opening up policy. In particular, since the beginning of the 21st century, with the gradual deepening of economic globalization, the economic and trade relations between China and Latin America have gained unprecedented leap – forward development. With the establishment and convening of the Sino – Latin American Forum in early 2015, and with the release of China's second policy document towards Latin America in 2016, the Sino – Latin American overall cooperation has formally entered a new stage of institutionalization.

The Sino – Latin American overall cooperation and the strategic essence of the construction of "the Belt and Road" are stemmed from the same origin, and the former is the natural and strategic extension of the latter. In particular, the construction in infrastructure fields (such as the ocean – to – ocean railway system), electric power, logistics and information channels has become a common consensus. Based on this, the Institute of Latin American Studies (ILAS) of Chinese Academy of Social Sciences (CASS), funded by the Academy's general project of the "Research on international risk of the Belt and Road and scope of cooperation expansion", combining innovative project research with the overall cooperation and international capacity cooperation in the series of domestic and foreign research. The research is divided into two categories in domestic and overseas fields. The domestic research is set for the important provinces which closely cooperate with LAC countries on "the Belt and Road", including six administrative divisions: the city of Beijing, and the provinces of Shandong, Gansu, Sichuan, Shanghai, and Guangdong. Overseas research is set for the two country groups: Russia, and Brazil and Peru. The Russian Latin American research think – tank has been maintaining close ties with China's Latin American scholars. Both Brazil and Peru are large Latin American countries, through which the ocean – to – ocean railways go, and both face such arduous development tasks as economic growth, social progress and structural adjustment. Therefore they are full of expectation for the economic cooperation with China, and are also relatively representative target countries for China's "going global".

By means of seminars, interviews, field visits and academic research, the research team has got a deeper understanding of the issues such as the overall cooperation, cooperation in capacity, in infrastructure, and of the economic and trade relations between the major provinces of China and Latin America. Four separate reports have taken shape. Ultimately, following breakthroughs have been gained in cognition by the research team: firstly, "the Belt and Road" and the overall cooperation between China and Latin America are in line with China's layout for diplomatic strategy; secondly, the Sino – Latin American integrated cooperation agrees with the docking needs of both sides in the economic restructuring and industrial development; thirdly, the overall cooperation between China and Latin America is conducive to the developing scope to seek mutual benefit in win – wining mode for both sides; and fourthly, the feasibility study on the early harvest from the "the Belt and Road" and the Sino – Latin American integrated cooperation can offer intellectual support for the in – depth development of the Sino – Latin American relations. On this basis, the research group has put forward four suggestions for the Sino – Latin American integrated cooperation. Firstly, China should act as the main promoter and contributor to overall cooperation, to facilitate early gains. Secondly, a synchronized drive should be realized in trade, investment, and finance, to promote achieving the goal of Sino – Latin American economic and trade cooperation. Thirdly, strengthen the Sino – Latin American cultural exchanges and enhance mutual understanding and awareness. And fourthly, coordinate the existing bilateral and multilateral cooperation mechanism, and build a network of multi – channel collaborative mechanism.

Key words: the Belt and Road; China and Latin America; integrated cooperation

In accordance with the spirit of CCP Eighteenth Congress and the "Thirteenth Five – Year Planning" framework, China will further advance her practice with Reform and Opening up Policy, and will continue to implement the "Going Global" strategy. China has proposed the initiative to jointly develop "Silk Road Economy Belt" and "21st Century Maritime Silk Road" (hereinafter referred to as "the Belt and Road"). This is an important measure for mutually promoting opening up internally and externally, better integrating attracting foreign investment and going global, and accelerating the cultivation of the new advantages in participating and leading international economic cooperation.

Latin America and the Caribbean area (hereinafter referred to as "Latin America") as a developing region with vast territory and large population, are the important fulcrums for the implementation of China's comprehensive opening up policy. In particular, since the beginning of the 21st century, with the gradual deepening of economic globalization, the economic and trade relations between China and Latin America have gained unprecedented leap – forward development. With the establishment and convening of the Sino – Latin American Forum in early 2015, and with the release of China's second policy document towards Latin America in 2016, the Sino – Latin American overall cooperation has formally entered a new stage of institutionalization.

The Sino – Latin American overall cooperation and the strategic essence of the construction of "the Belt and Road" are stemmed from the same origin, and the former is the natural and strategic extension of the latter. In particular, the construction in infrastructure fields (such as the ocean – to – ocean railways), electric power, logistics and information channels has become a common consensus. Based on this, the Institute of Latin American Studies (ILAS) of the Chinese Academy of Social Sciences (CASS), funded by the Academy's general project of the "Research on international risk of the Belt and Road and scope of cooperation expansion", combining innovative project research with the overall cooperation, international capacity cooperation and cooperation in infrastructure in the series of domestic and foreign research.

1. Literature Review and Phased Achievements

1.1 Literature review

In the past two years, the research literature on "the Belt and Road" strategy and "Sino – Latin American Economic cooperation" has gradually increased. In particular, the research on the Sino – Latin American overall cooperation has established a research path and framework for this research project.

1.1.1 About "the Belt and Road" strategy

Liu Weidong ("Scientific Understanding of the Belt and Road Initiative of China and Related Research Themes", *Progress in Geography*, 2015,Vol, 5) points out that the core goal of "the Belt and Road Initiative" is to promote orderly free flow of economic elements, efficient allocation of resources and in depth market integration, to promote a wider range, higher level, and deeper level of regional cooperation, together to create an open, inclusive, balanced, shared beneficial regional economic cooperation framework. The "the Belt and Road" framework contains a totally different concept from the past economic globalization, namely, "peaceful cooperation, opening and tolerance, mutual learning and understanding, mutually beneficial and win – winning", which is the embodiment of the cultural connotation of the Silk Road.

Lu Feng *et al* ("Why is it China? – Economic Logics of China's 'the Belt and Road Initiative' Strategy", *International Economic Review*, 2015 Vol.3) point out that "the Belt and Road Initiative" is a grand plan initiated by China to promote collaboration among countries in the vast areas between the countries of East Asia and the vast interior parts of Europe. China's initiated wide and systematic collaboration consists of policy coordination, infrastructure connectivity, trade promotion, funds accommodation and communication of people's sentiments. "The Belt and Road Initiative" serves as an integral part of China's new strategy to further opening up to the world in all fronts, prominently demonstrating a clear trend of more emphasis put on developing together with multitude of developing countries, conveying a new idea to make up the weakness of developing countries in economic growth by cultivating new global economic growth poles. The initiative shows benign interactive relations between the goals of open policy, diplomatic strategy, structural adjustment, and promoting growth. At present phase of development, China has comparative advantage in the capacity of conventional manufacturing and construction, and in opened macroeconomic area with endowment of huge size of national savings and foreign exchange reserves. By jointly constructing "the Belt and Road" China has a chance to demonstrate to the world that she is a dependable and capable cooperative partner with developing countries. In doing so, China will also benefit in wide fields in seeking shared development with multitude of developing countries.

Zhang Xiaojing and Li Liang ("The Belt and Road Initiative" and China's Export Trade in Perspective of Trade Facilitation, *Asia – Pacific Economic Review*, 2015,Vol.3) discriminate different measures of trade facilitation from different areas throughout the data of 45 countries from 2008 – 2013 and use the extended Gravity Model of Trade to identify the various impacts that the different levels of trade facilitation from different regions on China's exports. And they put forward relevant policy recommendations based on empirical results.

Xu Li ("Diplomatic Risk Faced by China's 'the Belt and Road' Strategy", *International Economic Review,* 2015,Vol.2) points out that "the Belt and Road" strategy faces three major challenges. The essence of the Asia – Pacific rebalancing strategy is not containment, but the defensive side of the two – sided betting strategy; the concerns of neighboring countries should be minimized as far as possible; China should note that "the Belt and Road" strategy has limited effect on transferring excess capacity and the security and benefits of foreign exchange reserves are hard to guarantee. It is necessary to divide the countries along the Belt and Road into four categories to deal with, focusing on the potential peripheral fulcrum country; for small and medium – sized countries in general only selective cooperation can be carried out; the need for a constructive approach to disputes over sovereign disputes; and for the bigger neighboring countries, special foreign policies should be formulated, starting with the economic and cultural field, establishing the "Asian Five Economic Forum", and establishing a "dialogue of Asian Civilizations".

1.1.2 About Sino – Latin American economic and trade cooperation

Sino – Latin American economic and trade cooperation has been a hot research topic in recent years. Overseas studies focus on the reasons, impacts and future prospects of the accelerated Sino – Latin American economic and trade cooperation. The focus of domestic research, however, is on the comprehensive cooperation under the "1+3+6" framework, especially on capacity cooperation, and constant attention is focused on the new prospects and new patterns of Sino – Latin American trade against the downward economic trend in Latin America, as well as the new extension of comprehensive Sino – Latin American cooperation under "the Belt and Road Initiative".

Espinasa, Marchán and Sucre (2015) focus their research on cooperation in energy and mineral fields between Asia (led by China and India) and Latin America. During 2000—2013, the trade volume of both sides in these two areas grew at an annual rate of 10.9% and reached $33 billion in 2013. High volume of bilateral trade has led many countries in Latin America and the Caribbean to shift their trade focus from traditional North America and Europe to East and South Asia.

Based on the above research results, Espinasa, Marchán and Sucre (2015) further discussed the investment of Asian enterprises in Latin America's energy and mineral interest rates. Their researches have shown that in the past 20 years, Asian enterprises led by Chinese and Indian ones have invested extensively in Latin American continent, covering energy enterprises, mines and farmlands. Analysis shows that while China's demand for energy and minerals may slow down over the next few years, for Asia as a whole, over the next decade, demands for energy and minerals will continue to present a rising posture – while China will always take an important position in the international energy market. Therefore, in the increasingly prosperous and stable development of Sino – Latin American economic and trade cooperation, to maintain the prosperity and stability of the new Silk Road will be the joint task of both China and Latin America.

Daniel E. Perrotti researched on the influence of China's economic growth to the export of Latin American Countries. He argued that China's economy and bilateral trade volumes with Latin America have both achieved remarkable growth. He predicted that the Chinese economy will remain at an annual growth rate of about 7% during 2014—2019, and that the total bilateral trade will maintain an average annual growth of about 10%.

Jin Xiaowen, in "Understanding Protests during Sino – Latin American Energy Cooperation", introduces the complexity of the domestic political environment in Latin America. By starting from protests during Sino – Latin American energy cooperation, the study shows that in the process of deepening Sino – Latin American energy cooperation, attention should be paid to the analysis of these protests, and the basic research of Latin America should be strengthened. In the mean time, publicity work should be well carried out to guard against possible risks during the cooperation.

Kong Qing – feng and Dong Hongwei, in "The Empirical Analysis of Impact of Latin American Trade Facilitation on China's Exports", systematically calculate the level of trade facilitation in major Latin American countries, then, by using the expanded trade gravity model to examine the influence of trade facilitation level on China's exports, they conduct a comparative study between the European Union and Latin American countries, and finally they separately examine the impact of the trade facilitation of the first – level indicators to China's exports to Latin America. The results show that China, on the basis of upgrading its own trade facilitation level, should strengthen her communication and cooperation with Latin American countries and jointly promote the trade facilitation level and facilitate bilateral trade development.

In Wu Tong and Chen Ying's "Risk Analysis on China's Direct Investment in Latin America's Major Countries", 9 representative countries are chosen for the research: Venezuela, Brazil, Argentina, Ecuador, Peru, Panama, Mexico, Colombia and Bolivia, which account for more than 90% of China's investment in Latin America. By establishing an evaluation indicator system, a quantitative analysis of the risks of China's direct investment in these countries, both politically and economically, has been conducted. The risk status in the 9 countries has been sorted with the view to providing a reference for subsequent investment.

In the aspect of "the Belt and Road Initiative" and extending integrated cooperation, Zuo Pin's discussion, in "Some Reflections on Construction of 'The Belt and Road' and Deepening Sino – Latin American Cooperation", focuses on the construction of "the Belt and Road" and the all – round cooperative relationship in the new period. The construction of "the Belt and Road" based on but not limited to the relevant countries along the ancient Silk Road, countries and international and regional organizations can also participate. Therefore, if Latin America can participate in the "the Belt and Road" in the future, it will play a direct role in promoting the all – round cooperation between China and Latin American countries. The research explores the emphasis of China's diplomatic strategy on Latin America at different periods and the misunderstanding on the current consideration towards Sino – Latin American Relations, analyzes the possibility and feasibility of the construction of "the Belt and Road" in Latin America, and finally, by thinking about the US policy on western hemisphere, explores its possible influence to the deepening of the Sino – Latin American Relations.

Besides, scholars at home and abroad have published monographs relevant to Latin America research, analyzing the issues of economic structure, social strata and institutional changes in Latin America from different perspectives. Among them, the relevant monographs include Jeff Dayton – Johnson's (editor – in – chief), "Latin America's Emerging Middle Class: an Economic Perspective", Schneider's "Industrial Policy Design in Latin America: Political and Commercial Relations and Neo – Developmentalism", Stuenkel and Taylor's (editors and authors) "Global Perspective of Brazil", Post, A.'s "Foreign and National Investment in Argentina: A Political Analysis of Privatization of Infrastructure", Needell, D. J.'s (editor and author) "The Rising Brazil: The Interpretation of New Global Power", Campello's "Latin America's Political and Market Rules: Globalization and Democracy", Santarcángelo, Justo & Cooney's (editors – in – chief) "Latin America after the Financial Crisis", Yáñez's "Latin America's Economy: New Measurement Data in History", Alston et al's "Brazil in Transformation: Faith, Leadership and Institutional Changes", Bagley *et al*'s (editors and authors) "The Colombian Political Economy in Background of 21st Century: From Mr. Uribe to Santos", Li Gang's "Institutional Changes and Economic Development: Institutional Analysis of Latin American Economic Development Model and Reform", and Hu Biliang's (editor – in – chief) "For a Common, Practical and Mutually Beneficial Development: The New Sino – Latin American Economic Cooperation Framework".

The most recent relevant reports include a series of books by ECLAC (editors – in – chief): "Inclusive Social Development: A New Policy for Eradication of Poverty and Reduction of Inequality in Latin America", "2015 Latin American Regional Trade Risks in world Economy: Judgment and Outlook", "2015 Survey on Latin American Economy: New Challenges for Revitalizing Investment Cycle", "Millennium Development Goals in Latin America: Regional Monitoring Report 2015", CAF – Latin American Development Bank's (editors – in – chief) "For A Safer Latin America: New Perspectives on Crime Prevention and Control", the Organization for Economic Cooperation and Development's (editors – in – chief) "(2015) Latin America's Economic Outlook: Development – Oriented Education, Technology and Innovation", etc.

1.2 Phased Achievements of the Research Team

On the basis of theoretical preparation and literature review, the research team has also done a lot of preliminary study work and has achieved fairly many phased achievements, mainly as follows:

Wu Baiyi ("Sino – Latin American Forum: The New Scenery of China's Great Power Diplomacy", *Qiu Shi*, 2015 Vol.3) points out that since the CCP's 18th Congress, the CCP Central Committee, led by general secretary Comrade Xi Jinping, has commanded both domestic and international situations, and constantly creatively put forward new diplomatic concepts, new propositions and new thoughts, according to the changes in objective situations. With the brave attitude of responsibility and the courage to put into practice, it actively explores the diplomatic path with China as a great power with her own characteristics. The first ministerial conference of the Sino – Latin American Forum was held successfully in Beijing, which once again presented to the world China's great power diplomatic theory and practice with her distinctive elements, style and spirits. The great power diplomacy with Chinese characteristics advocates the building of a new international relationship, which highlights the concept of "win – winning cooperation". Building a global partnership network is another important feature of China's diplomacy. The great power diplomacy with Chinese characteristics always adheres to the two advanced concepts of "inclusive growth" and "sustainable development". On the basis of the new changes in the situation at home and abroad and the new opportunities for development and cooperation in the process of adjusting to the world economy, China launches "the Belt and Road Initiatives" and more international public products for cross – regional cooperation, to implement the principle of being "true, real, intimate and sincere" so as to let the developing countries effectively benefit from cooperation, so that the multitude of Latin American and Caribbean countries can see the opportunities and hopes by embarking the Chinese development express.

Wu Baiyi and Shi Peiran ("Social Security and Trade Investment Environment: Existing Researches and New Possibilities", *International Economic Review*, 2015 Vol.3) point out that the conflict between the "subjective judgment" and "objective choice" in the convenience of trade and investment has been a common phenomenon, but it has failed to cause the academic thorough inquiry and theoretical amendment. None of the prevailing standards of measurement, assessment system and simplification index can adequately explain the diversified and constantly changing international trade investment practices. Their study discusses the relationship between social security and the environment of trade and investment from the existing social security measuring factors. By preliminary analysis it finds out the deficiency in existing social security measures, and puts forward the new variables of age structure of the investment target country, the profit model of the investor, the degree of political mutual trust between the countries, and cultural differences, in order to stimulate the debates among the peers, so as to promote the academic research on the relationship between social security and trade investment to a more in – depth, multidimensional and with more practically explanatory power.

Zhou Zhiwei and Yue Yunxia ("Sino – Latin American Overall Cooperation: Development Logic, Realistic Impetus and Future Direction", "*Latin American and Caribbean Development Report*" (2014—2015), Social Sciences Academic Press, May 2015) analyze the rationality and feasibility of Sino – Latin American cooperation, and consider it the inevitable choice of mutual dependence, mutual promotion and conscious self – improvement in the current global governance process. It consider such a phenomenon the natural process of the evolution of the relationship between the two sides, which is driven by the new external trend of South – South cooperation and global trans – regional cooperation, and is in line with the need of economic restructuring and docking. Based on President Xi Jinping's meeting with leaders of Latin American and Caribbean countries in Brasilia and the outcome document adopted by the First Ministerial Conference of the Sino – Latin American Forum, the study points out that the Sino – Latin American overall cooperation aims at achieving the goal of "five in – one" overall cooperation relationship, and five basic principles and directions need to abide by: firstly, adhere to the principle of equality and mutual assistance and strengthen the political mutual trust between the two sides; secondly, uphold the principle of mutual benefit and win – wining result seeking the upgrading of Sino – Latin American economic and trade cooperation; thirdly strengthen exchange and mutual learning and promote public diplomacy; fourthly, adhere to international cooperation to preserve common interests; and fifthly, adhere to the overall cooperation and promote bilateral relations. The research also emphatically studies the difficulties and obstacles faced by the Sino – Latin American cooperation, and emphasizes the need for the two sides to cope with the major challenges such as the complex geopolitical situation in Latin America, the differences in cooperation attitudes between regional countries, the complexity of the regional business environment, and the subtleties in countries without diplomatic relations with China. The study puts forward that in order to ensure the vitality and effectiveness of the Sino – Latin American overall cooperation, within short and medium terms three aspects of implementation approaches should be explored pertinently and be implemented at every level: firstly, build the "dual engine" drive of economic and trade relations; secondly, develop diversified public diplomacy channels; thirdly, consolidate relations with Latin American countries, regional organizations and sub – regional organizations, so as to effectively support the development of the overall Sino – Latin American cooperative mechanism.

Chai Yu ("Impact of FDI on Efficiency of Resource Allocation in Latin America and Industrialized Countries (Regions) of East Asia", *Journal of Latin American Studies*, 2015,Vol.2) has conducted a comparative study on the impact of FDI by transnational corporations within the region on resource allocation efficiency in Latin America and the industrialized countries of East Asia from 1950s to around 1990s. By adopting the method of counterfactual analysis, the study finds out that transnational corporations and their direct activities are only in the framework of the economic development strategy of the host country (region), which has an amplification effect on the utilization of local resources of comparative advantage. The host country (region) strategy, which meets the comparative advantage of resources, will promote the improvement of local macro – resource efficiency, otherwise will worsen this efficiency. TNCs proper would not have fundamentally reversed the direction of resource utilization in the host country (region). FDI has a significant negative impact on the efficiency of resources allocation and local enterprises in Latin America, but it has a promotion effect on East Asia. At present, there have been fairly big changes in TNCs' global resource allocation mode, and their requirement for the degree of refinement of economic governance is higher. In formulating economic policy different investment attracting targets, different industrial characteristics and different market competition situations should be distinguished, and emphasis should be laid to the effective coordinating between economic development strategy and policy.

Chai Yu, Kong Shuai and Li Shenggang's "Evaluation of Level of Tariff Concessions and Commitments for Non – Tariff Measures in Free Trade Agreements – A Study Based on Four Major FTA agreements by Colombia" studies on the four FTA agreements signed with the United States, the European Union, South Korea and Mexico by Colombia. The study gives quantitative analysis from the two aspects of tariff concessions and non – tariff measures in free trade agreements respectively, and has made the following conclusion: in the subsequent Sino – Colombian FTA negotiations, on the tariff concessions, China should lay emphasis on the sensitive field to Colombians such as negotiation on the field of agriculture; on non – tariff measures China should include in the FTA negotiations as many as possible the non – tariff measures, which China has no difficulty in implementation, and behavior of misuse of non – tariff measures should be avoided.

Zhang Yong's "Proposal on Development of Latin American Energy Resources Industry and Sino – Latin American Cooperation" (*International Economic Cooperation*, 2015,Vol.9), on the basis of sorting out Latin American energy resource reserves, sums up the industry's important influence currently on Latin American exports, revenue, investment contribution, society and environment. The study points out that China should take the three great opportunities in the period of price decline of international primary products, in Latin American regional integration, and in the gradual rise of new energy development to strengthen cooperation with Latin America in the field of energy, and in the meantime guard against potential risks in the cooperation with a pragmatic and cautious attitude.

Yue Yunxia's "Analysis of Aid to Latin America: International Status Quo and Chinese Model" (*Strategic Decision Research,* 2015,Vol.6) deems that while the United Nations Millennium Development Goals are fairly well achieved and the higher per capita incomes level reached, Latin America still faces two prominent problems of weak development capacity and poor stability, thus becoming a "key but non – core" area of international assistance, and the area has been receiving long term conditional support from traditional Western donors. In recent years, with the development of Sino – Latin American relations, China has risen to one of the important donor countries in Latin America. China's aid to Latin America differs from the western traditional model in guiding principles, implementation degrees, operation mode and mode of implementation, and also differs to China's model of assistance to traditional areas in Asia and Africa, which constitutes a beneficial supplement to the existing model, and has also brought in the Sino – Latin American win – wining situations. At present, the Sino – Latin American relations have entered a period of new strategic opportunity. It is necessary for China to expand the scale in the medium and short term, and further carries on the adaptability adjustment for "Latin Americanization" so as to consolidate her interests and potential benefits in Latin America.

Yan Zhimin's "The Roles Played by Three Categories of Actors in China's Engagement in Latin America" (*Journal of Chinese Political Science,* 2015, 20,Vol.3) analyzes the main functions and mutual relations between three kinds of actors in the Sino – Latin American economic cooperation: the governments, the enterprises, and the semiofficial organizations.

In summary, the above – mentioned literature and the phased achievements for "the Belt and Road" strategy and the study on Sino – Latin American overall cooperation have provided important theoretical preparation. However, from the viewpoint of theory with practice, information from government agencies, corporations, research departments and embassies in China and abroad reflects the actual business environments, cooperation status and problems. The results of researches aiming at these aspirations will provide solid empirical support for strategic and policy Studies.

2. Academic Value and Practical Significance

2.1 Academic Value

This research project has deepened the understanding academically of "the Belt and Road Initiative", the main academic value embodied being in the following respects:

Firstly, "the Belt and Road Initiative" is the strategic thought at present stage in China when the reform is being comprehensively deepened, and the new open economic system is being constructed. It is an important initiative to promote internal and external opening and mutual promotion, the better integration between attracting foreign investment and going global, and accelerating the cultivation of new competitive advantage in participation and leading the international economic cooperation.

Secondly, "the Belt and Road Initiative" relies on the existing bilateral and multilateral mechanisms and regional cooperation platforms of China and other countries to develop economic cooperative partnership with the relevant countries, with the aim of jointly building a community of common interests, destiny and responsibility, with political mutual trust, economic integration, and cultural inclusion.

And thirdly, the construction of "the Belt and Road" is in line with the strategic essence of Sino – Latin American cooperation. At present, Sino – Latin American relation is in the best period in history. The strategic framework for the comprehensive partnership between China and Latin America, by way of the Sino – Latin American leaders meeting in Brazil and the China – CELAC Forum in early 2015, was established. China and Latin America will build a new relationship in "five – in – one" pattern, with sincerity in politics, mutually beneficial in economic and trade cooperation, culturally mutual leaning and sharing experiences, close collaboration in international affairs, integrative cooperation, and mutual promotion, so as to create a Sino – Latin American community helping each other forward. The construction of "the Belt and Road" will endow new connotation and impetus for Sino – Latin American cooperation.

2.2 Practical Significance

This research project is the beneficial exploration of the cooperative scope for "the Belt and Road Initiative". The research conforms to China's overall strategy to raise the opening level, and is very important in practical significance.

Firstly, this research offers support to researches carrying out and implementing the second "*China's Policy Paper on Latin America and the Caribbean*". In 2008, the Chinese government proposed *Jointly Building a Comprehensive Partnership in the New Era*, and published the *China's Policy Paper on Latin America and the Caribbean,* the first policy document formulated by the Chinese government toward the region, and also a guideline of China's policy on Latin America. Eight years later, when President Xi Jinping ended his third visit to Latin America in November 2016, the Chinese government issued a second *China's Policy Paper on Latin America and the Caribbean*, which fully demonstrates the positive stance of China in the Sino – Latin American relations. This document is of great significance to promote the development of the Sino – Latin American relations.

As compared to the first document, the newly added highlights in the second paper focus on three aspects. The first is having established the goal of development for Sino – Latin American relations. The paper proposes that China is committed to building the "five – in – one" new pattern for the Sino – Latin American relationship. The second is having proposed the plan for promoting the integrative cooperation between China and Latin America. This document puts forward a clear plan for the next step of development for China – CELAC Forum, and states that the Forum Summit is to be attended by the leaders of China – CELAC member States when conditions are adequate. And the third is having enriched the scope for Sino – Latin American cooperation. The document puts forward 39 cooperative conceptions in 8 major areas: in politics, trade, society, culture, international collaboration, peace, security, judiciary, overall cooperation and tripartite cooperation, many of which are new areas. Therefore, the project can serve this policy document, which contributes to the implementation of China's Latin American policy.

Secondly, by "the Belt and Road" Initiative, China will actively promote her cooperation with related countries in construction of infrastructure, energy resources, capacity and equipment manufacturing, currency and market and other areas. The Sino – Latin American new framework of "1+3+6" cooperative model and the Sino – Latin American

"3×3" capacity cooperative model also clearly define these areas and modalities. In particular, the construction of infrastructure areas (e.g., the ocean – to – ocean railways) and the electric power, logistics and information channels has become a common consensus. At the same time, realizing the benign interaction between enterprises, societies and governments, extending fund, credit and insurance financing channels are also effective ways to implement "the Belt and Road Initiative".

And thirdly, the breakthrough of cooperation between China and Latin American countries is infrastructure construction and interconnection. The construction of the major infrastructure in Latin America, such as the ocean – to – ocean railways, does not only meet the need to reduce the regional transportation cost, enlarge the scale of trade, but also promotes the market docking and industrial docking, and promotes the development of RMB internationalization and trade investment facilitation. The construction of the Trans – Pacific Economic corridor linking Latin America and China can be an extension of "the Belt and Road Initiative".

Therefore, on the basis of the overall conception and the spiritual essence in the construction of "the Belt and Road", this research project relies on the Sino – Latin American overall cooperation plan, from the perspective of regional economic cooperation between China and Latin America, clarifies the attitudes, channels and roles of each of the market players such as the governments and enterprises. The research project has explored directions for solutions and concrete measures on establishment and improvement of market open system, trade investment promotion system, institutional guarantee system such as the legal system, and social responsibility system, etc.

3. Research Methods and Project Summary

3.1 Research Methods

Aiming at different research issues different methods have been adopted, mainly including:

1.Qualitative methods: including conference seminars, interviews, questionnaires, field visits, image data collection and so on. The project research team is divided into several groups, to visit "the Belt and Road" DRC, business offices, CCPIT, and other departments of important provinces, face – to – face interviewing relevant principals, and holding in – depth discussion on how shall "the Belt and Road Initiative" open the broad prospects for China and other countries in the economic cooperation. The overseas research groups talk with the government agencies, academic institutions and Chinese – funded enterprises to discuss the important significance of "the Belt and Road Initiative" and the ways to realize the further promotion of the Sino – Latin American overall cooperation.

2.Quantitative methods: The scientific conclusion will be obtained through data analysis and research for the problem that can be quantified. The aspects mainly include potentials in infrastructure project construction, economic and trade development trends, industrial docking capacity, and so on.

3.Countries (provinces) combine with regional research. In domestic research, attention is to be paid on the synergetic development problem in the region where the province is located. In overseas research focus should be on the relationship between country and regional integration.

3.2 Project Summary

The research is divided into two categories: domestic fieldwork and overseas fieldwork. The domestic investigation is set for the key "the Belt and Road" provinces which closely cooperate with Latin America, including six administrative divisions: the city of Beijing, and the provinces of Shandong, Gansu, Sichuan, Shanghai, and Guangdong. The research directions are preset to two categories. One is the research on government agencies, enterprises and think – tanks, the other is to do the talks and researches in the Latin American Embassies in China. Overseas research is set for the two country groups: Russia, and Brazil and Peru. The Russian – Latin American research think – tank has been maintaining close ties with China's Latin American scholars. Both Brazil and Peru are big Latin American countries, through which the ocean – to – ocean railways go, and both face such arduous development tasks as economic growth, social progress and structural adjustment. Therefore they are full of expectation for the economic cooperation with China, and also are representative target countries for China's "going global".

The overall steps and progress of the research are as follows:

From April to July 2015, preliminary research work was carried out in Shenzhen, Shandong and Beijing. At the same time, thematic interviews were carried out with major diplomats in embassies of Brazil, Chile, Peru, Colombia, Costa Rica and other Latin American embassies in China. During this period, the members of the project team made theoretical preparation and composed the relevant literature reviews.

In July 2015, research summary meetings and symposiums were held for the provinces to participate in early phase and major Latin American embassies, communicating information and experiences to lay a good foundation for the second phase of domestic and foreign in – depth research. At the same time, two foreign research group coordination meetings were convened jointly with foreign affairs departments.

From July to December 2015, the research groups traveled to the city of Shanghai and provinces of Gansu, Sichuan and Guangdong to conduct researches on institutions and enterprises. The research group members collated information and composed reports. In September, a survey on Russia was conducted, and in December the groups traveled to Brazil and Peru to carry out research on international capacity cooperation and the ocean – to – ocean railways.

In November 2015, a seminar on the results of periodic reports was held.

At the end of December 2015, final drafts were completed, other research results collated.

In 2016, the conference for general project summary was held.

This research project covers a wide range of scope and a long time span, but the results achieved are abundant. The part of domestic researches has mainly resulted in the information about the status quo, problems and the core demands of the participants. In the part of overseas researches, the research groups not only introduced to the object countries' governments, academia and business community China's "the Belt and Road Initiative", the Sino – Latin American new framework of "1+3+6" cooperative model and the "3×3" international capacity cooperative model, but also obtained first – hand research materials and data from the object countries' institutional discussions, seminars and the on – site visits relevant to the Sino – Latin American economic and trade cooperation and the ocean – to – ocean railways. These have offered abundant regional cases for the research projects of CASS on "International Risk and Cooperation Scope Development for 'the Belt and Road Initiative'".

4. Research Themes and Basic Conclusions

4.1 Theme One: Sino – Latin American Economic and Trade Relations and Status Quo of Capacity Cooperation

Since the beginning of the 21st century, Sino – Latin American relations have been foremost in economic and trade cooperation, and the cooperative forms have shifted from bilateral and multilateral cooperation to traditional cooperation and overall cooperation in parallel. By researches in cites of Beijing and Shanghai, and provinces of Shandong, Gansu, Sichuan, and Guangdong, the basic consensus has been formed: Sino – Latin American economic and trade cooperation has distinct phase characters and is currently undergoing the transition from "spontaneous" phase to "conscious" phase.

4.1.1 On the Content of Cooperation, Economic and Trade Cooperation Remains the Primary Concern of both Sides

Currently China has become Latin America's second – largest trading partner and the third largest source country of investment, and Latin America has become the largest overseas incremental market for Chinese products and capital in the last more than 10 years. The research shows that the various respondents in China and in Latin America are expecting a continuous expansion on economic and trade cooperation, while other forms of cooperation concerns are relatively invisible. The research deems that when both face the economic slowdown in the pressure and difficult circumstances, further strengthening the Sino – Latin American economic and trade cooperation can help China achieve the scale effect of advantageous capacity, alleviate the problem of imbalance in economic structure, and also benefit Latin America in improving infrastructure and in changing the singular economic structures. It is therefore an effective means to achieve win – winning situations for both China and Latin America, and will also be the cornerstone of Sino – Latin American overall cooperation.

4.1.2. On the Impetus of Cooperation, the Trade Motive Weakens and the Demand for Investment Cooperation Rises

Sino – Latin American economic and trade cooperation has long been dominated by trade, in parallel with development in investment and economy. Between 2000 and 2012, Sino – Latin American trade increase maintained an annual average of more than 30%, while investment growth was relatively slow. Nevertheless, since 2012, there has been a shift between the growth of trade and investment, and China's investment in Latin America has accelerated. The research data confirms that in the past more than 10 years, the volume of trade in the interviewed region has increased significantly, the increased proportion in the total amount of trade accounted for 3% to 9%, but the recent trade volume with Latin America is relatively stable or even shows a small downward trend. This shows that by complementary trade exchanges, Chinese enterprises have completed or initially completed the "spontaneous" type of development in Latin American market. Some enterprises have begun to seek modes of optimizing their resource allocation, through investment to "consciously" explore the potentials of Latin America, and to maximize the regional market gains.

4.1.3 On the Cooperative Motivation, the Market and the Resources Are the Main Motivation

The fieldwork shows that in the area of trade, the concentration ratio in Sino – Latin American trade structure is fairly high, the region interviewed mainly imports iron ore, metal products, agricultural by – products, paper pulp and integrated circuits and so on; Latin America has become one of the large – scale markets of Chinese manufactured goods, the main exports of the region interviewed are machinery, electronic products, garments, textiles, chemical preparations and hardware tools etc. The trade products and regional industrial structure of each region interviewed have a high degree of integration, and the resources and market complement are largely formed in Latin America. On the investment aspect, the choice of investment destinations of the enterprises in the region is tendentious, consumer products such as electronic and electrical appliances manufacturers choose the scale markets of Brazil, Argentina and Mexico with a market orientation; and metallurgical, petrochemical and other resource – based products manufacturers will choose Peru, Brazil, Chile, Venezuela and Bolivia and other resources with a resource – orientation.

4.1.4 In Partnership Positioning, Latin America Has Become a Key Market for 5 Categories of Chinese Products and Capacity Investment

The first category is the agricultural and mining industry products, which are needed by Latin American competitive industries, such as pesticides for farming and agricultural machinery equipment and equipment for petroleum exploitation. Latin America is the key area for China to export the relevant products and to make relevant investment. The second category is China's advantageous manufactured goods, such as consumer electronics products and medical equipment. China's products and technology in Latin America takes a fairly large market share. The third category is emerging industries, such as new energy vehicles, which are not infiltrated by US and European standards, and China's products and capacity in Latin America have a certain technological advantage, becoming a catalyst for industry standards and market access rules, and Latin America has thus become an important global demonstration market. The fourth category is the market especially adaptable for Chinese model, such as infrastructure projects and large – scale electromechanical equipment. By Two Optimal Concessional Loans or financing lease, China offers Latin American buyers financing support or loaning construction, thus ensuring her market share, forming a mutually beneficial cooperation. The fifth category is the new commercial activities characterized by "Internet + ", with online or offline trade, with integration between investment and logistics, shortening the distance between the product supply and demand. This will maximize the long – distance export earnings of agricultural and sideline products, with strong Latin American market adaptability, thus becoming the emerging investment areas for Chinese enterprises.

4.1.5 In the Cooperative Policy Effect, the Bilateral Preferential Policy Dividend Manifests, while the Trade Effect Exceeds the Investment Incentive

Since 2005, China has successively signed the FTA with Chile, Peru and Costa Rica. The fieldwork verifies the trade creation effect by the FTA, and the three big free trade zones have a significant influence on the trade flow. To all the respondents, Chile and Peru are in the top ten Latin American trading partners, and Costa Rica has also become one of the main import and export objects of Shanghai Municipality and Sichuan Province. Meanwhile, however, the FTA has not yet yielded significant capital concentration effects on the distribution of investment destinations.

Therefore, in the New Normal phase of China's economy, Latin America is expected to become the supplier of China's resources, energy and intermediate products; the receiver of her superior products and capacity, the implementer of her innovative technology and standards, the important collaborator of her overseas economic strategy, and the stakeholder to China's economic interests. Sino – Latin American cooperation contributes to the promotion of linking each other's industrial chains, forming a new value chain division, promoting the diversification of the trade structure, and driving the efficient running of three major engines of trade, investment and financial cooperation, to achieve a comprehensive upgrade of Sino – Latin American economic and trade cooperation. To this end, the research group considers that the focus may be laid on the following aspects:

Firstly, building an enterprise – based overall cooperative platform.

The asymmetric reality of the willingness and ability of the two sides in the Sino – Latin American cooperation pattern determines that China should lead the top level design of Sino – Latin American cooperation, constructing the mechanism and framework for the overall cooperation, and creating favorable conditions for future overall cooperation. Therefore, it is the fundamental guarantee for better cooperation with Latin America and the future deepening of Sino –

Latin American cooperation that the governments coordinate, build the overall cooperation platform for enterprises, formulate via consultation the development strategy of the Sino – Latin American cooperation, and constantly expand the scope of bilateral FTA. It helps alleviate the problem of "latent transaction corpus vacancy" in Sino – Latin American cooperation, and also helps to cope with the weak governance capability of Latin American governments. This platform integrates infrastructure construction, import and export, and financial services organically, and contributes to put the enormous potential of cooperation on a firm footing.

For example, the construction of the "ocean – to – ocean railways" in Brazil could bring about a series of industrial upgrades, in whose process China's infrastructure industry, financial industry, trade and industry, and a variety of services may be benefited in this round of construction and industrial chain reengineering process. In such a process, a higher level of cooperation platform transcending enterprise level will contribute to resolving Latin America's problems similar to construction of infrastructure in public – private partnership (PPP).

Secondly, perfecting comprehensive information exchange and service platform for enterprises.

A diversified, specialized and comprehensive enterprise information service platform is the important safeguard to further strengthen Sino – Latin American economic and trade cooperation. Recently, the Chinese Ministry of Commerce launched a "public service platform for going global" capable of providing enterprises with the basic information and risk situation of the investment destination. On this basis, it is necessary to combine the demands of Chinese – funded enterprises, to organize the "going global" enterprises to share experiences and lessons, to summarize the needs of different enterprises, and to report the typical problems and policy issues to Chinese and Latin American government departments. The realization forms of the above – mentioned information cooperation can be diversified, not only by cooperation with domestic and foreign research institutes, but also by cooperation with the embassies of Latin America, and also by cooperation with various types of enterprises, in order to ultimately build a multi – participation, professional, comprehensive information exchange service platform.

Thirdly, constructing the mechanism of avoiding Latin American exchange rate risk.

Due to the facts of large volatility in currency exchange rate of many Latin American countries and of limited coverage by Sino – Latin American currency swap agreements, the integration of innovative financial services has become the primary task for avoiding financial risks. China should strive to promote the cooperation between Chinese – funded banks, insurance companies, and guarantee companies etc., to attract financial service institutions such as the National Bank of Latin America into this area. This will help not only to circumvent the dollar settlement, but also, to a certain extent, to circumvent the exchange control of Latin American countries, it will also be conducive to promote the establishment of local currency swap agreements, and help promote such agreements for the import and export services by Chinese enterprises. In addition, this initiative will help shorten the settlement cycle, shorten Latin America's approval cycle for the cooperation projects (Latin American countries' dollar settlement project often needs congressional approval with a long process), and further advance the construction work of offshore market and liquidation market.

And fourthly, straightening out the mechanism and promoting the administrative efficiency.

China's state – owned enterprises are the backbone of the current Sino – Latin American economic and trade cooperation, but the existing management system of the state – owned enterprises does not fit into the target of strengthening the overall cooperation. There is an urgent need to improve in two aspects: the first, to improve the existing separate operation mechanism. For example, under the separate operation system, in a typical public – private partnership (PPP) infrastructure construction work, such as the commodity for service, the deal will not occur because of the separation of service provider and the beneficiary; and the second is to improve the current profit assessment index. The typical characteristics of Latin American economy are strong in periodicity and the large in currency fluctuation. The rational coping behavior should be: purchasing the high – quality resources, technology and enterprises in Latin America when their currency value sharply drops, and energetically developing export to Latin America when their economic growth is in good state. Such a strategy has been commonly adopted by the United States and other countries. But under China's current short – term profit appraisal index, enterprises are more likely to devote to the realization of short – term goals.

In terms of administrative efficiency, the central and local governments should fully consider the needs of enterprises in customs clearance, tax rebate and so on, to shorten the cycle of process. It can be considered that experiments be carried out in each Free Trade Zone (FTZ) to integrate the import and export formalities, further reduce the various approval items, realize the policy simplification, and change the serious lag regulation. In addition, the governments should play a role in two aspects: the first is to establish coordination and rights protection mechanisms, to provide support for enterprises; and the second is to guide enterprises to adopt more appropriate strategies in different cyclic phases.

4.2 Theme Two: Challenges and Aspirations Faced by Sino – Latin American Overall Cooperation

The fieldwork has discovered that the Sino – Latin American overall cooperation reflects the political wills of the two sides to deepen cooperation. The cooperation has the basis and impetus for continuous advancement. However, as a new cooperative mechanism, the overall cooperation is still in the initial stage, the internal pressure from running – in and external sensitivity factors are the major challenges that still need to confront with.

Firstly, the geopolitical environment in Latin America is complex. The environment in Latin America is generally stable, but there are still many complicated factors. In the first place, the region has not yet fully resolved the problem of delimitation of territory and territorial waters between a few individual countries. In the second place, U.S. adjustments of her Latin American policy have made the geopolitical environment in the region more complex. And in the third place, other foreign powers have become new variables in geopolitical politics in Latin America.

Secondly, there are differences in the aspirations by Latin

American countries to the Sino – Latin American overall cooperation. The positions of Latin American countries are very different in view of the Sino – Latin American overall cooperation. Comparatively, Mexico, Chile, Peru, Colombia, and Costa Rica responded positively to the initiative of the overall cooperation, because these countries take "opening the market, strengthening cooperation with the Asia – Pacific region, and integrating into the Asia – Pacific production chain" as the priority goal in their international cooperation, and the Sino – Latin American overall cooperation is not only consistent with their strategic orientation to strengthen cooperation with China, but will also open up the channels to connect Asia The most complex attitudes are from Brazil and Argentina. While Latin American countries have a relatively coherent political will to establish a Sino – Latin American cooperative mechanism, there are inevitably different political orientations in the process of concrete cooperation, thus increasing the coordination difficulties for the parties, and even bringing uncertainty to the anticipated early harvest.

Thirdly, it is under larger pressure to achieve the Sino – Latin American trade goals. Between 2002 and 2012, the rapid economic and trade growth of Sino – Latin America was based on the rapid growth of both economies. In the last two years, with the slowdown of economic growth in both sides, coupled with a sharp fall in commodity prices, the growth of Sino – Latin American trade has been weak. Objective analysis shows that there exists a big gap between the current situation of Sino – Latin American bilateral trade and the potential growth rate required for the "ten – year goal". And the elimination of this gap is still facing three major challenges: the first is the lack of demand due to the economic downturn in both sides; the second is the price pressures arising from the persistent downturn in commodity prices; and the third is the "ultra – capacity" problem of the local market caused by over – speed growth in the early period.

Fourthly, it is of certain difficulty to further increase the investment in Latin America. The cooperation plan states that in the next ten years, "the stock of investment of both sides reaches at least 250 billion US dollars". In the light of current situation, this objective faces double pressure due to the change in the global environment. One pressure comes from the investment impetus. Since 2015, the economy in Latin America has experienced a downturn, and there have been phenomena of serious "negative growth, high inflation and high unemployment rate" in Brazil and Venezuela, China's key investment countries. As a result, management of enterprises faces practical difficulties, and willingness for further investment is suppressed. The other pressure comes from the business environment. In terms of the three major categories of evaluation indicators, business facilitation, productivity environment nurturing and industrial supporting capacity, the region's global rankings are poor. The bottleneck factors are mainly embodied in the high tax standards, poor financing availability, limited government governance capacity, inadequate infrastructure supply, imperfect labor market, inadequate industrial collaboration and support, which have inhibited the enthusiasm of external capital.

Fifthly, there are sensitive factors from countries without diplomatic relations with China. At present, the countries without diplomatic relations with China amount to 24, while Latin America accounts for 12. In the course of overall cooperation with Latin America, China should deal with these factors with caution. In the first place, the factors of non – diplomatic relations will directly affect the communication and coordination between China and countries without diplomatic relations. In the second place, the Sino – Latin American overall cooperation, including countries without diplomatic relations, could trigger a ripple effect on the cross – Taiwan Strait relationship. When the cross – Strait relationship strained, the degree of influence by the factors of countries without diplomatic relations would be greater and might form a "counteractive" to cross – Strait relations. From this point of view, the "countries without diplomatic relations" and "Taiwan factors" will inevitably become the two important variables in the Sino – Latin American cooperation in the short and medium terms.

At the same time, our research also shows that Sino – Latin American cooperation in the short term will not only face a variety of risks, but also face limits by various institutional constraints.

4.2.1 The risks posed by cyclical factors in Latin America. Latin America's overall industrialization capacity is limited, while the first and third industry proportions are fairly high, and their export structure is dominated by primary products. The above mentioned characteristics of Latin American countries account for their generally poor economic independence, and vulnerable to the influence of global economic cycle. The dual factors of economic cycles and financial cycles are intertwined to form the characteristics of alternating fluctuations in exchange rate, inflation and wage growth in Latin America. The research shows that since 2013, Latin America has experienced economic slowdown, inflation intensified, and currency devaluation intensified in Brazil, Argentina, Venezuela and other major economic and trade partners. These have formed negative impacts on the economic interests of enterprises, and on China's export and investment confidence.

4.2.2 The risks posed by Latin American policies. Latin American has a relative advanced labor and environmental legislation standards, and because of historical debt crisis, their control on foreign exchange is rather strict. The research shows that their current policies mainly cause three types of potential risks to the management of Chinese enterprises: the first is the risk of profit repatriation. Due to foreign exchange control implemented in countries like Argentina, China – funded enterprises generally report that it is very difficult to remit their profit. The second is the labor risk. The number of Latin American skilled labors is rather insufficient, and the labor protection standard is high, often showing characteristics of "a weak government and a strong trade union", and the government's decisions are manipulated by interest groups. Many enterprises interviewed state that they encounter certain difficulties in employment in local areas, or encountered strike crisis. And the third is the risk of environmental conflict. In Latin America, both environmental legislations and the standards are high, non – governmental environmental protection organizations are powerful, and there exists the conflicts with Indian aboriginals on eco – environmental issue, which increase the uncertainty for the entry of foreign capitals, and in some of the enterprises interviewed their planned investment projects hence have ended in failure.

4.2.3 There is deficiency in Latin American business environment. The overall business environment in Latin America is under institutional constraints, and the enterprises interviewed state five kinds of problems: the first, the high cost of regional production in labor, logistics, taxation, and other apparent or obscure costs; the second, in most countries the establishment of new companies is time – consuming during complex process; the third, the social security situation is poor, with violent crime rate more than double of other regions; the fourth, the cycle for obtaining a visa is generally longer in the region, and many countries need the "counter – signed visa" procedure, which constitutes a heavy blow to the timeliness in the bilateral cooperation; and the fifth, there is certain randomness in policy formulation and implementation, a typical example being Argentina's emergency import quota provisions, which exacerbates the uncertainty in the local investment and trade for Chinese – funded enterprises.

4.2.4 Constraints and limitations in "Going Global" policy. Some of the current policies show inadequate support to Chinese enterprises in Latin America's operating activities, or even restrict corporate behavior. The first is the financial constraint. The enterprises in the "going global" process are constrained by the existing financial system, so that their financing is both costly and difficult. There is a need for further adjustment to the financial policy innovation. The second is the personnel constraint. The examination and approval process is too long for the business trip project, and the stipulated time interval to visit Latin America is too short, which have become an obstacle of foreign cooperation and exchange. And the third is the supporting constraint. At present, the domestic supporting policy measures serving enterprises' "going global" relatively lag behind, not conducive to cope with the risks posed by the rapid implementation of the Sino – Latin American overall cooperation strategy.

4.2.5 The absence in transaction subject. Due to the poor infrastructure of Latin American countries, the export capacity of many resources – rich countries suffers severe restrictions. They expect China to invest on construction of roads and port facilities, but such expectations are difficult to come true in the traditional model of individual enterprises as transaction subjects. Latin American governments cannot afford a huge amount of construction costs, which can only be covered by the signing of export agreements such as agricultural products and resources. Such phenomena have been commonplace in Latin America. The Sino – Latin American economic and trade cooperation begins to confront with the problem of the absence of potential cooperation subject after the spontaneous phase by the enterprises.

In addition, from September 7 to 11, 2015, the delegation of ILAS–CASS visited Russia for academic visits and exchanges with the Latin American Institute of the Russian Academy of Sciences, the Latin American Bureau of the Ministry of Foreign Affairs, the Russian Strategic Research Institute, the University of Moscow, the University of the Russian People's Friendship, and other government departments and research institutes. The exchange results show that China and Russia have a great opportunity to further deepen strategic partnership. Both sides believe that the cooperation over Latin American affairs and the policy coordination by China and Russia must be carried out under effective framework. In summary, the views of both China's and Russia's government departments and the think – tanks can be implemented in the following three frameworks:

Firstly, the cooperation framework of BRICS. Russia has always considered "BRIC" as a key tool for multilateral diplomacy, hoping to build it into a comprehensive strategic collaborative mechanism. In her view, Latin America has a higher degree of recognition of "BRICS", and the regional countries take it as an important international factor. This mechanism can integrate the regional powers such as Brazil to directly collaborate with China and Russia to achieve the integration of the three powers, which can not only enhance the influence of China and Russia in Latin America, but also be conducive to divert the West in the geopolitical strategy.

Secondly, the cooperation framework of the APEC. Currently, there are only 3 Latin American members in the Organization (Chile, Mexico and Peru). Many Latin American countries are eager to join in. Therefore, China and Russia should promote the organization's admission to more Latin American members. In terms of the present stage, the agenda of APEC has a strong Asian color, and the accession of more Latin American countries will enhance the degree of the Organization's attention to the needs of Latin America, thus making it more balanced on its agenda. It will also be a platform for policy co – ordination by China and Russia with Latin American countries on the Pacific Rim.

Thirdly, the cooperation framework of the "Sino – Latin American Forum". The scholars and policy makers of Russia believe that China and Latin America have established a new mode of cooperation through the "China – CELAC Forum", and the party is willing to promote cooperation with the parties of China and Latin America with the help of this channel. The Sino – Russian cooperation in this regard is very important to the political and economic fields in Latin America. However, the research team has noted that the Russians have great doubts about Community of Latin American and Caribbean States, considering that the political symbolism of the organization is greater than the practical effect, and the organizational structure has great limitations, its imperfect mechanisms make it difficult to react swiftly and effectively to the changeable international situations. Views from the Russian Trip conclude that the Rio Group, the predecessor of the Community of Latin American and Caribbean States, is more capable of reaching agreement and implementing actions. Thus, on the one hand, Russia is politically supportive of the integration process of the Community and Latin America, but still take a foothold in bilateral cooperation for resolving practical problems, as bilateral relations are easier to coordinate, more pragmatic and efficient; on the other hand, Russia intends to use China's experience for reference and build a framework of cooperation with Latin America in future, similar to the Sino – Latin American cooperation forum, to enhance the level of relations with Latin America.

4.3 Theme Three: Aspirations and Expectations relating to the Ocean – to – ocean Railway Project

From November 29 to December 7, 2015, the investigation team of ILAS – CASS visited Brazil and Peru. This was the international research by the Latin American Institute under the Academy's general research project framework of the "Research on international risk of the Belt and Road and scope of cooperation expansion", and it was also the first formally organized research by ILAS on the construction project of the "ocean – to – ocean railways" in Brazil and Peru. The main views of the Peruvian scholars are as follows:

Firstly, the construction of the ocean – to – ocean railways is of great significance to Peru, Brazil, China and Latin America. As a developing country, China's infrastructure development provides a model for Latin

American countries. Peru's industrial and infrastructural development is at the margin, and transportation has a fundamental role in promoting the development of a country and in improving its competitiveness. Compared with European and American countries, Peru's logistics cost is too high, while the integration of railways, ports and highways is conducive to reducing logistics cost, promoting the mobility of passengers and cargo, improving the situation of imbalanced regional developments, adjusting the highly concentrated development model in Lima, and promoting the planting of soybean in the remote regions of the Midwest of Brazil, and promoting the construction of copper mines in the Andes in Peru. This is a project that has a significant impact on the future of Peru.

Secondly, according to the feasibility study of the project, the ocean – to – ocean railways are based on the amount of cargo transported by Peru and Brazil to achieve the sustainable operation of the railways. In consideration of different geographic forms of coastal, mountain and tropical rainforests in Peru, while the construction of the ocean – to – ocean railways includes the integrated construction of a variety of transport modes such as seaports and railways so as to achieve more effective concentration of goods, this requires the cooperation of central and local governments to make overall planning and construction. In view of the previous experience in railway and road construction, the existing problem in the aspect of franchising is the specific conditions in the contract concerning property rights, maintenance, operation and management, which require coordination and communication between the two sides as they involve the joint management and guarantee of the construction and operation of the railways by Brazil and Peru. In addition, in the area of technical cooperation and personnel training, China will undertake the task of training railway construction personnel and technicians.

Thirdly, a lot of feasibility study needs to be done in the aspect of environmental protection. The ocean – to – ocean railway routes pass the Amazon area, and finally across the Brazilian border into Peru, and reaching the ocean shore in Peru's Port of Callao, or Mollendo, or Arica. Whether the Amazon Rainforest area, the living areas of Indian communities and villagers, may suffer from the environmental damage and impact still needs a lot of studies, and relevant laws, standards and management measures need to be formulated with the participation of planning by civil society and indigenous communities, so as to mitigate the environmental and social adverse effects of the project. It also requires effective cooperation between Peru and China to promote the economic development of Peru.

Fourthly, attention should be paid to the evaluation of the ocean – to – ocean railway project. Peru, as a developing country, needs to attract investment to promote her own development, but attracting international investors cannot only focus on economic effects and cannot undermine social development and cause environmental destruction. Therefore standards are needed to assess the direct and indirect impacts of investment projects, the kinds of measures investors will take in building infrastructure, and whether they also promote the mobility of society, reduce costs, maximize the use of resources, rather than just mining resources, so as to improve the efficient use of resources. Investors and Peruvians should be complementary for common development. In addition, risk assessments need to be emphasized. The formulation and implementation of the project should be accomplished jointly by all participants, both directly and indirectly. Risk research is conducive to reducing the social conflicts arising during the process of the project, and to focus on the impact or benefit of the Indian groups and other groups involved in the project. Regional management also deserves attention. The ocean – to – ocean railways will run through different regions, there are differences in the characteristics, geology and biological characteristics in these areas, therefore biologists and relevant personages should be invited to participate in the effective management of the relevant areas.

Fifthly, it is necessary to let scholars play a positive role in the ocean – to – ocean railway project, which they presently have little knowledge of the specific situation. The ocean – to – ocean railway project has been participated by the public sector, the private sector, technicians and different stakeholders, but as the project is so significant and complex that it is not only an infrastructure project but also of political significance. Scholars should be more involved, offering advice, holding forums, discussing and exchanging views, and providing policy advices. Peru's upcoming general election result in April 2016 will affect the development trend of the project. Whether the next government will incorporate this project into the government agenda, it still requires further information after the election.

Sixthly, the ocean – to – ocean railway project may be viewed from a strategic perspective. The ocean – to – ocean railways may open the doors for Peru to the countries of South American and the Pacific countries, not only their cargos can concentrate on Peruvian ports, but goods from other countries can also be attracted for transport by this railway. This is not only a railway, but also a maritime route connecting China. This project is of great significance and is also an important project for the integration of infrastructure in South America, initiated by the Union of South American Nations. Under the framework of the integration of infrastructure in South America, a series of infrastructure projects will be in operation in the next 10 years, and the ocean – to – ocean railways are among the top priorities for the development of the region as a whole.

5. Breakthroughs in Understanding and Policy Recommendations

5.1 Breakthroughs in Understanding

The research team has carried out domestic and foreign researches guided by the classical theories of International Industrial Specialization, International Trade, International Investment, Regional Development, International Relations etc. On this basis, the following breakthroughs in understanding have been achieved:

First, "the Belt and Road" and the overall cooperations are in line with the layout of China's diplomatic strategy. 2015 is the year when China comprehensively advanced her power diplomacy with Chinese characteristics. China's international influence has been entirely promoted, in global politics, economy, security and other fields she has put forward a series of initiatives and programs with wide – ranging and far – reaching impacts, accelerating the deepening of relations with the major countries, and injecting new vitality and impetus for the neighboring countries, in the Middle and East Europe, in Africa and in

Latin America developing countries, and even in the uncertain world economy. The Sino – Latin American overall cooperation is an important part of the diplomacy with Chinese characteristics, and is one of the important objectives of realizing the comprehensive layout of China's diplomacy, and of docking the development strategy of all the countries. It is also one of the important carriers of China practicing her diplomatic idea of the human destiny community.

Second, the Sino – Latin American integrated Cooperation conforming to the economic restructuring and industrial development of the docking needs of both sides. After recent over 10 years of economic and trade integration, the Sino – Latin American economies have formed a close relationship. At present, as the two sides are both in the stage of economic restructuring and transition, the economic cooperation between the two sides also need to move towards quality growth, and reconstruction in pattern and connotation. The new structural complementation has emerged, requiring further cooperation between the two sides to further establish consensus and priority implementation routes.

On the one hand, China's existing advantages capacity and surplus capacity meet Latin American actual needs in line with her requirements for industry diversification and product value chain moving upward. With the "new normal" economy, China continues to increase the scale of foreign investment, through capital and industrial integration, to offer her surplus capacity to the world: traditional products such as steel, cement, textile etc., newly developed products such as photovoltaic and wind power, and high – end equipment like high – speed rail and nuclear power. The industry and product structure of most countries in Latin America is not quite perfect, and infrastructure construction has yet to be improved, therefore, there is an urgent need to introduce substantial investment to diversify the industrial structure. With the expansion of China's overseas investment scale, in 2014 China's investment to foreign countries exceeded the scale of foreign investment in China for the first time, becoming a net exporter of capitals. And China's foreign economic cooperation has been transferring from the original mainly commodity output to capital output. Therefore, there is a fairly big scope for Sino – Latin American industrial cooperation, and there are conditions for further deepening the industrial docking and fusion. On the other hand, with China's domestic demand – driven strategy, the transformation of domestic consumption patterns and capabilities offer a huge potential market for Latin American goods and services. With basically ending of the imitation type consumption wave, China's public consumption mode tends to individuation and diversification, it is imperative that the supply system be open, the development diversified, and the imported goods, services and overseas consumption be increased. Therefore, the need of the linkage of Sino – Latin American industrial chains and the change of demand structure will help to form new investment and trade growth points, and promote the increase of bilateral cooperation level and expand the cooperation scale.

Third, the Sino – Latin American overall cooperation is in favor of seeking mutually beneficial development space. Just as the national conditions in countries along route of "the Belt and Road", there are great differences between Latin American countries and China in cultural traditions, ideology, and institution and mechanism. Based on the understanding of the diversity of the member states of the Community of Latin American and Caribbean States, the cooperative mechanism of Sino – Latin American integrated cooperation takes the "two – wheel driving" strategy, which is mutually reinforcing and complementary "multilaterally" and "bilaterally". The parties can jointly agree on key areas and projects of cooperation in the framework of the Forum and relevant sub – Forum fields, and carry out pragmatic cooperation in various forms so that the Sino – Latin American integrated cooperation and the bilateral cooperation between China and the member states of the Community of Latin American and Caribbean States run in parallel and are mutually complementary.

Meanwhile, the promotion of Sino – Latin American overall cooperation is bound to take full account of the host country's own development aspirations and strategies. Based on the full understanding of the existing advantages, development directions and constraints of the host country, the research has explored the space and field for economic and trade cooperation with host countries, on the one hand to refine the three main engines, six major areas and the concrete content of the 3×3 cooperation model; and on the other hand, further tap the cooperation potential, broaden the channels, and lay a good foundation for future

Sino – Latin American cooperation.

Fourth, the feasibility study on the early harvest by "the Belt and Road Initiative" and the Sino – Latin American integrated cooperation can provide intellectual support for the in – depth development of the Sino – Latin American integrated cooperation. For nearly a year, there have been effective advances on "the Belt and Road Initiative" and the Sino – Latin American integrated cooperation. The Sino – Latin American Forum has established a new sub – forum in the fields of agriculture, infrastructure, energy mining, economy, industry, scientific and technological innovation, and social policy. Both China and Latin America have shown a good momentum of expanding the cultural exchanges. The First Sino – Latin American Political Party Forum was convened successfully at the end of 2015, the sub – forums for youth politicians, local governments, and think – tanks, are also in active preparatory probing process. These preliminary results mean that the possibility of the early harvest of the Sino – Latin American integrated cooperation is increasing. In general, these help promote the creation of the "upgraded edition" for the Sino – Latin American integrated cooperation on the momentum, which helps to enhance China's power of advocacy and influence in the process of the integrated cooperation.

However, due to the pressure and influence from external development environment, and due to the differences in the development structures, levels, and the cooperation capabilities of both sides, there exist certain difficulties for the Sino – Latin American Cooperation to achieve a batch of early harvest in projects with wide economic and social "overflow effect". To this end, it is not only the common concern of the governments and enterprises in both sides but also the interests and responsibility of the academia to seek the approaches for the Sino – Latin American integrated cooperation to gain early harvest and the field of its distribution, to find the path, practical effect and future prospect of such harvest, and to explore the major crux obstructing such the early harvest and find out the coping strategies.

5.2 Policy Recommendations

Through research and investigations, the research team believes that the Sino – Latin American overall cooperation is focusing on the long – term system arrangement, and attentions should be laid on the rhythm control of the gradual deepening of the promotion and implementation of cooperation, to achieve effective collocation of short – term, medium – term and long – term goals. In the short and medium terms, the policy thinking of Sino – Latin American integrated cooperation can proceed from the following aspects:

Firstly, China should act as the main promoter and contributor to the integrated cooperation, facilitating early harvest.

In the current stage, there are certain differences in aspirations for the integrated cooperation between China and Latin America and among Latin American countries. Especially, in the Sino – Latin American integrated cooperation, the Latin American counterpart, the Community of Latin American and Caribbean States, is not a political entity but a political agreement reached by the countries of the region on the integration of Latin America, and it has no permanent secretariat. Therefore it cannot produce a substantive binding resolution, which also has many restrictions in the implementation. Therefore, the Community of Latin American and Caribbean States is still difficult to play the leading role in the mechanism of the Sino – Latin American overall cooperation, and at this stage, China should give more play in the initiative and take more responsibility accordingly, so as to promote this cooperation mechanism to achieve early harvest and phased achievements to strengthen the centripetal force of the mechanism, laying the foundation for its sustainable development. To this end, based on the development needs of both sides, China should be guided by the opening concept in the "Thirteenth Five – Year Planning", linking up the current "the Belt and Road" and other important strategies, undertaking the role of the public product provider in the Sino – Latin American integrated cooperation, and by promoting the construction of the interconnection facilities in Latin America expanding the common interests of both sides, and eliminating the restriction of infrastructure in regional integration, enhancing the joint force of the Community of Latin American and Caribbean States, and promoting the formation of its symmetric status and function in the overall cooperation.

Secondly, achieving the synchronized drive in trade, investment

and financial to promote the goal of Sino – Latin American economic and trade cooperation.

Economic and trade cooperation is the realistic foundation and advancement platform for the Sino – Latin American integrated cooperation, and it is also the areas with most contents in the "Cooperative Planning" established in 2015. Over the next period of time, in the aspect of trade, the marginal expansion of both volume and kinds of products for import and export should be promoted to break through the downward pulling effect of bulk commodity prices, so as to cater to the common needs of both China and Latin America for the industrial upgrading and transformation, and promote the benign upgrading of Sino – Latin American trade. In terms of investment, on the traditional basis of energy resources, infrastructure and agricultural cooperation investment shall be increased in manufacturing and infrastructure, and promote the real progress of the Sino – Latin American capacity cooperation, so as to make investment a new growth point of Sino – Latin American economic and trade cooperation. In the financial aspect, by using the platform of the Sino – Latin American integrated cooperation, the Sino – Latin American capacity cooperation fund and the Sino – Latin American cooperation fund should produce full effect; the deepening of cooperation by both sides in settlement in local currency, and in joint financing, the needs for Sino – Latin American trade and investment upgrading can be better served, and the basis for strengthening Sino – Latin American cooperation in global currency system reform can be established. This will also serve China's need for RMB internationalization and Latin American need for financial stability, and provide a basis for strengthening Sino – Latin American cooperation in the global currency system reform. On the whole, promoting the formation of multiple – driven economic and trade cooperation between the two sides is the realistic path for realizing the 10–year goal of economic and trade cooperation, and is also the inevitable route for promoting the deepening of economic and trade cooperation.

Thirdly, strengthening cultural exchanges and promoting mutual understanding and cognition.

Compared with the rapid advancement of the Sino – Latin American economic and trade, the mutual cognition and political trust of the two sides are apparently insufficient. In particular, strengthening cultural exchanges should become the cooperation project in medium and short terms for cultivation of continuous strength. By multi – channeled cultural exchanges mutual cognition and understanding can be strengthened and the foundation for the Sino – Latin American integrated cooperation can become solid. Based on the understanding of the status quo of the Sino – Latin cultural Exchange, the policies to be considered are: (1) Strengthening the "window" function in Confucius Institutes; (2) Realizing the institutionalization of Sino – Latin American think – tank exchange; (3) Strengthening the interaction between the think – tank and the governments and enterprises; (4) Strengthening the "bridging" role by foreign residents from both sides; and (5) Strengthening exchanges between local governments.

Fourthly, coordinating existing bilateral and multilateral cooperation mechanisms, building multi – channeled collaborative mechanism network.

Although both sides of China and Latin America have activated a mechanism for overall dialogue and cooperation, the foundation and core content remain the bilateral relations between China and Latin American countries, and the relationship between China and Latin American regional organizations and sub – regional organizations. At the starting phase, the bilateral relations between China and Latin American countries and the relationship between China and Latin American regional organizations are especially important pillars supporting the Sino – Latin American integrated cooperation. In addition, the "Sino – Latin American Forum" is the overall cooperation mechanism beyond the bilateral relations, and the cooperation content and mode are jointly negotiated and decided by a number of participating countries, this differs from the principle of "complementary of each other's advantages" in bilateral cooperation, and, under the framework of overall cooperation, the relevant participating countries may have direct competitive relations in certain areas and certain specific cooperation projects, and the solutions, to a certain extent, depend on the bilateral level of negotiations. Therefore, under the integrated cooperation mechanism, on the one hand, it is necessary to promote the smooth operation of the cooperative mechanism of the Sino – Latin American integrated cooperation through coordination with key countries, on the other hand, it also needs to be through bilateral channels to coordinate the unavoidable conflict of interest, so as to avoid the overall cooperation be influenced by the partial competition.

And because the integration of the Sino – Latin American integrated cooperation is on the basis of the integration of Latin America and the Caribbean, China by utilizing the established dialogue mechanisms (such as the dialogue mechanism established with the Rio Group in 1990, the dialogue mechanism established with the MERCOSUR in 1997, and consultation mechanism established with the Andean Community in 1999, and so on), has supported the regional integration processes of the Community of Latin American and Caribbean States, the MERCOSUR, the Andean Community, the Caribbean Community, the Rio Group, the Alliance of South American States, the ALBA, and the Pacific Alliance. China, on the one hand, promotes the stable development of integration mechanisms in Latin America and the Caribbean, and on the other hand, can formulate reasonable and meticulous regional cooperation arrangements in line with the characteristics of the sub – regions, realizing the convergence and mutual promotion from all aspects.

Report One

Cooperation between China and Latin America: Overview, Opportunities and Challenges

Zhou Zhiwei and Yue Yunxia

In January 2015, the first ministerial meeting of the China – Latin America and the Caribbean Community Forum (referred to as the "China – Latin America Forum") was held in Beijing. The three major documents adopted at the meeting outlined the principles, approaches and mechanisms of this forum. The overall cooperation between China and Latin America therefore has been officially institutionalized.

Latin America and the Caribbean (often briefly referred to as Latin America) have distinctive characteristics regarding geopolitical landscape, regional integration, economic and social development and so on. These factors not only explain the reason why Latin America is the last place to be integrated into China's global strategy for cross – regional cooperation, but also become the fundamental elements to be taken into consideration when we explore the future of the overall cooperation between the two sides and make specific plans regarding cooperation with this region.

In order to comprehensively understand the China – Latin America Forum as well as the cooperation between China and Latin America, it is necessary to analyze not only the fundamental realities and the driving forces from an academic approach, but also take a broader perspective to clearly identify the challenges faced by the overall cooperation between the two sides. Based on these judgments, we can thus establish targeted policies and specific measures in accordance to the characteristics of Latin America.

1. Fundamental Realities and Driving Forces for the Overall Cooperation between China and Latin America

Since the beginning of the 21st century, China – Latin America relations have moved onto the "fast lane" with rapid development. The two sides have formed a favorable environment in which rapid economic and trade growth promotes all – round cooperation between China and Latin America. In this process, bilateral ties between China and Latin American countries have been significantly strengthened. China and regional organizations in Latin America have also established permanent mechanisms for consultation and dialogue. At the same time, the two sides now have more shared interest and larger common ground in the global governance. With bilateral relations continuously growing stronger, the China – Latin American cooperation model is now ready to "shift gear". Besides, both China and Latin America share the pursuit to bring the cooperation to a higher level. Therefore, the overall cooperation between the two sides has now been efficiently transformed from "vision" into "reality."

From the perspective of policy priority from both sides, there are sufficient realities as the foundation for the overall cooperation between China and Latin America.

First, Latin America is an important part of China's comprehensive strategy of cross – regional cooperation.

In China's foreign policy and strategic outlook, South – South cooperation has long been a priority. With its growing overall national strength and international influence, China has shown stronger initiative in South – South cooperation. While China always abides by basic principles such as equality, mutual benefit, win – win cooperation and common development, China now has strengthened its exploration of new models of South – South cooperation in the new era and carried out a series of practical cooperation with developing regions to achieve cross – region cooperation so as to "both save diplomatic resources and improve the efficiency of cooperation". In more than a decade, China has initiated the establishment of the China – Africa Cooperation Forum, the China – Arab Cooperation Forum, the "10 + 1" and "10 + 3" mechanism with ASEAN, the China – Central Asia Cooperation Dialogue, the Shanghai

Cooperation Organization and other mechanisms for cooperation and dialogue. After the new administration took office, China attaches extra importance to a "community of common destiny" developing countries puts forward view of the balance between justice and profit.

Latin America is a region with a high concentration of developing countries, thus in the new era becomes the "new frontier" on which China's diplomacy is actively developing. In the past decade, China has not only "attached extra importance to Latin America from a strategic perspective", but also launched a comprehensive planning of policies regarding this region. In November 2008, China issued *China's Policy Paper on Latin America and the Caribbean* for the first time, delivering a signal for China's overall cooperation with Latin America. In June 2012 at UN Economic Commission for Latin America and the Caribbean (ECLAC), then – Premier Wen Jiabao proposed the initiative to "establish a forum for China – Latin America cooperation". In July 2014 at Brasilia, President Xi Jinping joined the first meeting with leaders of the Latin American countries. He proposed to form a "community with common destiny "Between the two sides and establish a five – in – one relationship featuring political mutual trust, win – win outcome in economic and trade cooperation, learning each other in people to people exchange, close cooperation in international affairs, and synergy between overall cooperation and bilateral relations.

In January 2015, the first ministerial meeting of the China – Latin America Forum was held, which marked the "initiative to reality" of the overall cooperation between the two sides. November 2016, President Xi Jinping paid his third trip to Latin America and China timely released its second *Policy Paper on Latin America and the Caribbean*. All those events laid a solid historical foundation to build the Community of Common Destiny between the two sides, and outlined the general picture of the comprehensive China – Latin America cooperation in a top – to – down manner. The overall cooperation between China and Latin America has helped to achieve full coverage of the overall cooperation between China and the world beyond, especially in developing regions. From the overall mechanism for cooperation between China and foreign countries/regions, the overall cooperation between China and Latin America is a "must – have" in China's global strategy, which is in line with China's policy of cross – regional cooperation as a whole.

Second, China is a priority for the "Pacific Strategy" of Latin American countries.

With the world's political and economic focus shifted to Asia and the Pacific, economic cooperation around the Asia – Pacific region has become the highlight of the current international relations. Driven by this trend, Latin American countries have significantly increased their strategic focus on the Asia – Pacific region. In particular, as China's overall national strength grows, its leadership in global governance becomes stronger and great potential of economic and trade cooperation gets tapped and unleashed, Latin American countries have therefore prioritized China's when setting their diplomatic policies. "China Opportunity" and "Pacific Consciousness" have become an important consideration for the foreign strategy of this region.

For most Latin American countries, the importance of China is not only reflected by the huge demand for primary products and raw materials, but also by China's as new positioning and role as a global power of capital investment. Many Latin American countries see China as an important source of financing for both raising restructuring funds and obtaining urgent yet low – interest loans.[①]

In addition to realistic economic considerations, strengthening the partnership with China is also in line with the geopolitical interest of Latin American countries such as diplomatic diversity and independence of foreign policies to counteract the regional dominance of the United States.[②] Because of this, many Latin American countries have been re – designing their policies with China. In 2008, the Brazilian government

① Agustín Lewit, "Una Nueva Geopolítica: China – América Latina", *Centro Estratégico Latinoamericano de Geopolítica*, enero 7 de 2015. http://www.celag.org/una – nueva – geopolitica – china – america – latina/ (date of research: Jan. 22nd 2015).

② Shannon Tiezzi, "China's Push Into 'America's Backyard'", *The Diplomat*, February 08,2014. See the link: http://thediplomat.com/2014/02/chinas – push – into – americas – backyard/: Jan 12th 2015.

issued the "China agenda"①. Brazilian think tanks called for "developing systematic and specific policy regarding China"②. In 2009, the Chilean government launched the "China Policy Plan". Mexican President Pena also stressed that "the two countries can build an economic relationship that opens the door to a new era of economic complementarity".③ In addition, it is worth emphasizing that China's diplomacy champions a series of new concepts of international development such as the "openness and inclusiveness" concept of cooperation, the view on the balance between justice and profit, and the initiative of building a community of common destiny with the vast number of developing countries. The moral appeal helps to build stronger confidence of the Latin American countries to deepen their cooperation with China.

In conclusion, China – Latin America's overall cooperation has its own inherent logic. It is an inevitable result of strategic adjustment on the basis of the consensus on comprehensive and pragmatic cooperation between the two sides on the basis of the two sides of the. At the same time, China – Latin America's overall cooperation also has its inherent driving forces which will support its sustainable development and continuous growth. Only by recognizing these endogenous momentums can we evaluate the future development of China – Latin America's overall cooperation in a long – term and objective perspective, especially to avoid misjudgment due to temporary economic difficulties and third – party factors.

From a broader perspective, several factors serve as the inherent driving forces for the overall development between China and Latin – America:

① Including the Ministry of Industry, Development and Foreign Trade, the Ministry of Foreign Affairs, the Ministry of Agriculture, Forestry and Reclamation, the China – Brazil Entrepreneurs Committee and the National Federation of Industry http://www.cebc.org.br/pt – br/projetos – e–pesquisas/projetos – realizados/agenda – china/agenda – china – acoes – positivas – para – relacoes(date of research: Jan 10th 2015).

② Roberto Abdenur, "Quem precisa da China", *Cebri Textos*, 2011, http://www.cebri.org/midia/documentos/texto06.pdf.(date of research: Oct. 20th 2014).

③ Fu Zhigang: "Mexican President Peña wrote the article praised the relationship between Mexico: the future of the common future of the ancient country", "Guangming Daily" , June 5, 2013, 008 version.

First, the rapid – growing development of relations between the two sides lays the basis for the overall cooperation between China and Latin America.

Since the 21st century, China – Latin America relations have achieved rapid development thanks to the highly complementary and mutually reinforcing economy.

On the political front, China has established various types of strategic partnership with Brazil, Argentina, Chile, Peru, Venezuela, Mexico, Costa Rica, Venezuela, Ecuador and other Latin American countries. The strategic mutual trust between the two sides has also been improved significantly. At the same time, "summit diplomacy" between China and Latin America has been accelerating through bilateral and multilateral channels. Since taking office, President Xi Jinping and Premier Li Keqiang have visited Latin America to release China's political will to strengthen cooperation with Latin America.

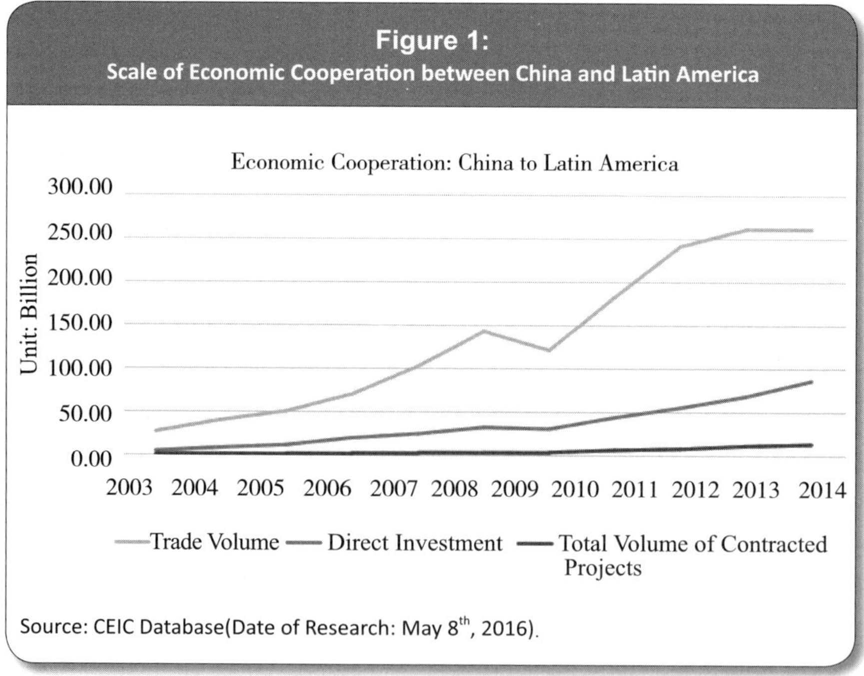

Source: CEIC Database(Date of Research: May 8th, 2016).

On the economic front, a rapidly enlarging scale of economic and trade is the most significant part of the development of China – Latin

American relations (see Figure 1). In the ten years between 2003 and 2012, Latin America became the fastest – growing region in China's foreign trade, with bilateral trade volume increased by more than 30% annually. Since 2013, China has remained as the second largest trading partner in Latin America despite a lower – growth in China – Latin America trade. Latin America is also the fastest – growing region for China's outbound investment. From 2003 to 2014, China's direct investment in Latin America increased from 4.6 billion USD to 106.1 billion USD (12% of the total outbound investment), with an average annual increase of nearly 30%. At present, China is one of the leading sources of investment in Latin America while Latin America has become China's second largest overseas investment destination.

Economic cooperation is also an important part of China – Latin American cooperation. In 2014, China's contracted projects in Latin America completed a turnover of 13.2 billion USD (accounting for 9.3% of the total), sending 25,106 employees abroad (8.6% of the total) Latin America has become China's third largest overseas engineering market after Asia and Africa.①

When it comes to mechanism – building, China has basically established institutional strategic dialogues with all major countries in Latin America: China and Brazil have established a high – level coordination and cooperation committee; with Mexico and Argentina respectively, China has set up a standing committee for cooperation; China and Venezuela have set up a high – level mixed committee and the China – Venezuela Cooperation Fund; China and the Caribbean have established China – Caribbean Economic and Trade Cooperation Forum; and so on. At the same time, China has signed free trade agreements (FTA) with Chile, Peru and Costa Rica, and launched a joint feasibility study on the FTA with Colombia.

In multilateral cooperation, China has successively become an observer of regional integration organizations such as Inter – American Development Bank, the Latin American Integration Association, the Organization of American States (OECS), the Economic Commission for Latin America and Caribbean (ECLAC), the Pacific Alliance and so on.

---

① CEIC Database for the Chinese Economy (date of research: May 8th 2016).

China has also established dialogues with the Rio Group, the Federation of Southern Cities and the Andean Group. We have further established consultation mechanisms with major Latin American countries at the ministerial level. Therefore, China has already formed a multi – channel and complementary network of coordination mechanism.

In order to implement the initiative for overall cooperation, China and Latin America have carried out a number of attempts in recent years such as exchange mechanisms including the China – Latin America Entrepreneurs Summit and the China – Latin America Think Tank Exchange Forum and other dialogues including the China – Latin American Young Politician Forum and the China – Latin American Agriculture Ministers Forum. Based on the current level of China – Latin America relations and the existing cooperative mechanisms, both sides are ready for considering an overall planning of China – Latin America cooperation.

Second, complementarity of economic transformations from the two sides serves as a new engine for the betterment of the overall cooperation between China and Latin America.

At present, China and Latin America are facing varying degrees of economic restructuring and transformation. Different from the past cooperation model driven by complementarity and with trade as its core, today's economic interaction between China and Latin America is being reconstructed. First of all, the "going out" campaign of Chinese enterprises is in line with the needs of Latin American countries to diversify their industrial sectors. Under the economic "new normal", China has also increased the scale of foreign investment to promote the "going out" of surplus and competitive capacity through the combination of capital and industry. Highlights of China's foreign investment include traditional surplus production capacity such as steel, cement, textile tec., emerging surplus production capacity such as photo – voltaic and wind power, as well as high – end equipment such as high – speed railways, nuclear power and others.

At the same time, Latin American countries have very similar industrial structures with each other while their products are rather less diversified. Poor infrastructures are in dire need of restructuring and upgrade through investment. Therefore, there exists potential feasibility of effective docking between the two sides in the industrial transformation. Secondly, the shift in China's consumption patterns provides a huge potential market for Latin American goods and services. The Chinese market is now ready to provide a diversified market for Latin American exports, changing its over – concentrated trade with China. The industrial chain docking of the two sides and the changes in China's demand structure contribute to the formation of new investment and trade growth point, which will further support the overall cooperation.

Third, economic and trade cooperation between China and Latin America has reached a new stage and calls for stronger and broader cooperation between the two sides.

Economic and trade cooperation is not only the most active part of China – Latin American relations, but also has been one of the driving forces behind the development of bilateral relations. However, after more than ten years of rapid development in the early period of this century, the economic and trade cooperation between China and Latin America has entered a transitional period. Its core features are threefold:

First, complementary cooperation based on comparative advantage is becoming sluggish China's export showed varying degrees of "saturated" state in major regional markets especially Brazil, Argentina and so on. Trade friction takes places in more fields. Secondly, Chinese enterprises are no longer making investment in and extensive way like the early years but turning to a global layout directed by the value chain. Thirdly, investment and trade facilitation has become a key factor influencing the promotion of China – Latin American economic and trade cooperation.

It can be seen that China's economic and trade cooperation with Latin America is shifting from "being spontaneous" to "self – consciousness", resulting in higher requirements for policy coordination and integrated development arrangements between China and Latin America. This requires substantial cooperation and "early harvest" so as to further expand the scale and improve the level of economic and trade cooperation.

2. Contemporary Challenges for the Overall Cooperation between China and Latin America

The overall cooperation between China and Latin America reflects the political will of both sides to deepen cooperation and has the basis and impetus for continuous promotion. However, as a new cooperative mechanism, the overall cooperation between China and Latin America is still in its infancy. It is still facing immense and immediate challenges from both internal coordination and external sensitivity. Therefore, the two sides need to put more emphasis on the quality and sustainability of the overall cooperation rather than one – sided pursuit of the speed of advance. For the decision – makers, they have to make objective judgments on the challenges faced by the overall cooperation between China and Latin America. This is the only way to make targeted and sustainable policy planning and cooperation design.

First, the geopolitical landscape in Latin America is intricate.

Latin America's overall environment is stable, but there are still many complex factors.

First, some countries in the region have not yet fully addressed the territorial delimitation both on land and at sea. For example, in Central America, the border issues still exist between Nicaragua and Honduras, between Guatemala and Belize and so on. Territorial and maritime disputes remain unsolved in the Andean region among countries like Venezuela, Colombia, Suriname, Guyana and others. Among Bolivia, Chile and Peru, there is a territorial dispute involving Bolivian Estuary. Chile and Peru are still arguing over maritime delimitation. In addition, Argentina and the UK still have the decades – long sovereignty dispute over the Malvinas. Tensions emerge from time to time.

Second, as the US adjusts its policy towards Latin America, the geopolitical landscape in this region has become even more complicated. In November 2013, US Secretary of State Henry Kerry officially declared that "the door of the era of Monroe Doctrine has ended". He stressed that "the relationship between the Americas should be established on the basis of equal partnership and common responsibility"; in July 2015, the United States officially restored diplomatic relations with Cuba. In March 2016, Obama visited Cuba and "right – turned " Argentina. Those logically – coherent measures release a strong signal that "US now attaches more importance to the policy towards Latin America". In particular, as the current left – wing forces in Latin America is on the decline, more frequent interactions are to come between the United States and Latin America. The overall cooperation between China and Latin America is more and more likely to be influenced by this factor.

Besides, other foreign powers become the new variables in geopolitics in Latin America. Over the past decade, India's relations with Latin America have increased significantly, especially with Brazil. The two sides have strategic dialogues which covers many important current global governance issues. Those mechanisms include the BRICS, the Four Countries①, the India – Brazil – South Africa Forum, the Group of Four, and the trade and finance giant "G20". India held its first foreign ministers' meeting with the Latin American Troika in August 2012 and began to build a series of bilateral cooperation mechanisms aimed at building a strong tie with this untapped land and make Latin America its brand new partner for cooperation. ②

Russia's presence in Latin America has also increased significantly. In November 2008, then – Russian President Dmitry Medvedev declared Russia's policy of "returning to Latin America" in a high – profile. In May 2013, Russia and the Latin American "troika" held a foreign ministers' meeting and planned to develop it into a "permanent political dialogue and cooperation mechanism", aiming at reversing its decline in the influence upon Latin America.③ In addition to the emerging powers, the EU and Japan have also increased their policy making on Latin America. The EU and Latin America have held three summit summits to achieve the integration of the mechanism with the EU – Latin American Summit (established in 1999). Similarly, Japan has expressed the idea of establishing a dialogue mechanism with the Latin American community, strengthening the coordination of the two sides in many areas.

It can be seen that there are many complicated variables in the

---

① A temporary group including Japan, Germany, Brazil and India with the attempt to become permanent members of the UNSC.

② Ashok B Sharma, India to host India – CELAC Dialogue, *The Indian Awaaz*, July 11, 2012. http://theindianawaaz.com/index.php?option=com_content&id=8338 (date of research: Jan 20th 2015).

③ Ivan Nechepurenko, Russia seeks to restore influence in Latin America, The Moscow Times, May 30, 2013, http://in.rbth.com/world/2013/05/30/russia_seeks_to_restore_influence_in_latin_america_25591.html (date of research: Jan 16th 2015).

geopolitical environment of Latin America, especially as the United States strengthens the policy of Latin America and the cooperation between foreign powers and Latin America is becoming more institutionalized. China will not only face more complicated competition in Latin America but also is likely to face a Latin America that asks higher offer in a "balance strategy" among all the major powers.

Second, each Latin American country has its own pursuit against the backdrop of the overall cooperation between China and Latin America.

In view of the overall cooperation between China and Latin America, the position of the Latin American countries are quite different. Comparatively, Mexico, Chile, Peru, Colombia, Costa Rica and other countries respond positively to the overall cooperation initiative, as these countries regard "open markets, strengthened cooperation with the Asia – Pacific region and integration into the Asia – Pacific production chain" as their international cooperation priorities. Accordingly, the overall cooperation with can strengthen their strategic cooperation with China and open up the channel to connect the Asia – Pacific market.

Cuba and Ecuador have showed great enthusiasm on the main platforms of the overall cooperation between China and Latin America, "China and Latin America Forum". Cuba, in particular, played a very important coordinating role in promoting the acceptance of China's "China – Latin America Forum" initiative by the Community of Latin American and Caribbean States. Ecuador's main expectation of the "China – Latin America Forum" is to seek economic assistance, develop trade and investment, and strengthen scientific and technological cooperation with China.

Similarly, the Latin American countries that have not established diplomatic relations with China also welcome the overall cooperation. The overall cooperation mechanism of China and Latin America has provided an opportunity for these countries to strengthen cooperation with China, both to get rid of the plight of "taking sides" and to help them to maximize their own interests.

On the contrary, Caribbean countries and Venezuela have different thinking with the countries mentioned above. They have a strong yet one – way dependence on China with corresponding cooperation mechanisms such as China – Caribbean Economic and Trade Cooperation Forum, the China – Venezuela Cooperation Fund. As a result, they worry that the overall cooperation will weaken China's economic attention with them.

Brazil and Argentina have the most complex attitudes. Argentina's economic situation has been poor in recent years while protectionism is a big concern. Besides, its bilateral relations with China in recent years encountered some obstacles. As a result, this country doesn't show much enthusiasm for the overall cooperation yet it does not want to miss this opportunity either.

Brazil has a strong mixed feeling regarding this initiative: on the one hand, Brazil recognizes that with the expansion of China's economic strength and overseas interests, China's efforts to increase cooperation with Latin America is an irreversible trend. While infrastructure is the crux focused by the current bilateral cooperation, the overall cooperation between China and Latin America will help the upgrading of infrastructure in Latin America and promote the integration of infrastructure in the region. This trend is consistent with the Brazilian policy objectives such as "regional connectivity" and "market integration". On the other hand, China's expansion in Latin America will not only compress Brazil's market space in the region, but may also weaken Brazil's leadership, which is quite the opposite with its regional strategic thinking and geopolitical interests.

Although the Latin American countries have a relatively consistent political will in establishing the overall cooperation mechanism of China and Latin America, there will be inevitably different policy orientation regarding specific cases of cooperation. As a result, it becomes even more difficult for coordination and even brings uncertainty for our early harvest.

First of all, due to differences regarding economic and social development, cooperation needs and cooperation capacity, the integration of Latin American countries still faces obstacles. Coupled with differences in their demands for China, the early driving forces for this mechanism should come from the Chinese side, which will bring even the stronger pressure than that of the early part of China – Africa cooperation.

In addition, unlike the African Union acting as a parallel counterpart with China, the Community of Latin American and Caribbean States is a young regional organization. It is at an early stage with its institution building, coordination capability and integration capacity being immature. With the development of the Pacific Alliance and the MERCOSUR, the "East and West" division in South America has increased. In addition, the diversification of national interests and aspirations in the Latin American region will be a major problem in the future development of the China – Latin America Forum. For example, the Pacific countries hope that through the "China – Latin America Forum" mechanism they can further integrate themselves into the Asian production chain, and even to establish a free trade mechanism with China, reflecting a certain "pull into Asia" strategic direction. In the current Latin American regional policy, these countries rarely regard "Latin America" as a whole, which goes against the inner concept of the "China – Latin America Forum" to put the Community of Latin American and Caribbean States as a starting point.

Third, considerable difficulty still exists for achieving the trade goals between China and Latin America.

From 2002 to 2012, the development of China – Latin American economic and trade is based on the rapid growth the economy on each side. In the past two years, with a slower growth of the economy on both sides and a sharp drop of commodity prices, China – Latin American trade growth is becoming sluggish. According to statistics from the China Customs, after a slight increase of 2 consecutive years, the China – Latin American trade experienced a sharp decline of 10.3% in 2015. In the first quarter of 2016, year on year decline further expanded to 16% (Figure 2)①.

The "cooperation plan" adopted at the first ministerial meeting of the China – Latin America Forum established the goal of "reaching a total trade volume of 500 billion USD in the next 10 years". According to this target, between 2015 and 2024, trade between China – Latin American

① CEIC Database for the Chinese Economy(Date of Research: May 8th 2016).

must score an average annual growth rate of 6.6%. Based on objective analysis, there is a big gap between the goal and the reality of the bilateral trade between China and Latin America. The elimination of this gap is still facing three major challenges: the lack of demand caused by the economic downturn, long – lasting downward pressure of commodity prices, and the premature growth caused by the "ultra – capacity" problem of the local market.

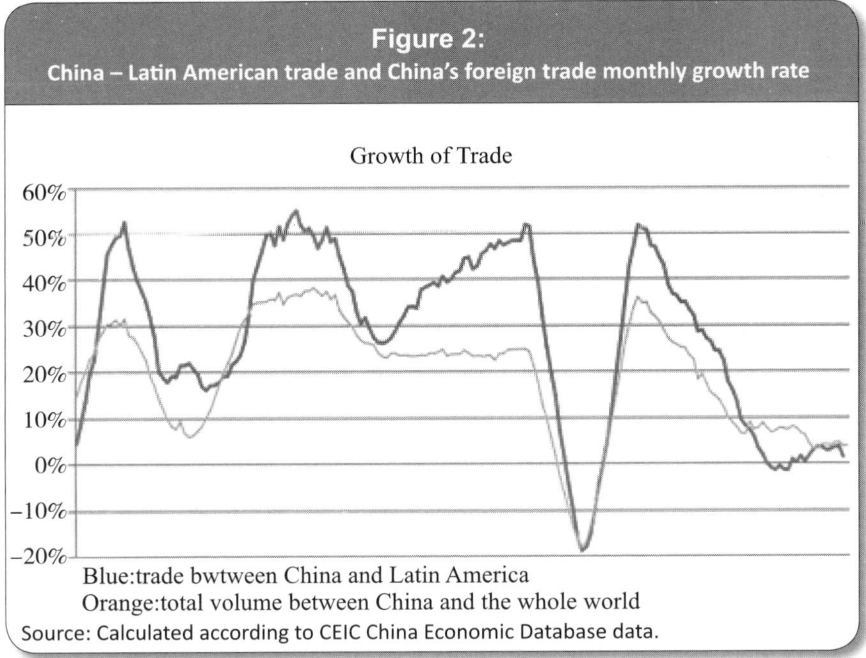

Figure 2:
China – Latin American trade and China's foreign trade monthly growth rate

Source: Calculated according to CEIC China Economic Database data.

Although the China – Latin American trade target is not a binding indicator, it is directly related to the efficiency and sustainability of the overall cooperation between China and Latin America because of its important weight in the current China – Latin American relationship assessment system.

Fundamental changes are not likely to happen regarding the difficulties in both economic downturn and structural transformation from the two sides. Both China and Latin America need to have a clear understanding of this challenge. When necessary, we have to make appropriate adjustment of the pace and targets of cooperation, or to find a new growth point of cooperation between the two sides.

Fourth, China and Latin America also face obstacles to expand mutual investment.

Investment is one of the three major engines of the new framework of "1 + 3 + 6" cooperation[①] between China and Latin America. It is also one of the main channels to realize the new mode of "3 × 3"[②] regarding capacity cooperation between China and Latin America. It is the focus of the future development of the overall cooperation. As pointed out in the Cooperation Plan, the two sides will "reach a bilateral investment of at least 250 billion USD".

Under this goal, both sides are facing greater pressure. However, China has greater obligation to realize this goal because significant asymmetry exists for the bilateral investment between China and Latin America: China's investment in Latin America is much larger than Latin American investment in China, and the potential of the former is relatively large. In the extreme case of assuming that[③] China fulfills all its commitments, the average annual increase in China's investment in Latin America should exceed 11.2% over the next decade.

However, from a realistic point of view, changes in the global environment make this goal facing double pressure. First, enthusiasm

---

① "1+3+6" is the China – Latin American cooperation framework proposed by Xi Jinping at the meeting of leaders of China – Latin America and the Caribbean held in Brasilia. This framework includes: ONE plan to achieve inclusive growth and sustainable development as the goal; THREE engines (trade, investment, financial cooperation) as the driving force to promote the comprehensive development of China – Latin American cooperation, to achieve a scale of 500 billion US dollars of China – Latin American trade in the next 10 years, to achieve 250 billion US dollars of Chinese investment in Latin America, and to promote the expansion of bilateral trade and local currency exchange; SIX specific areas including energy resources, infrastructure construction, agriculture, manufacturing, scientific and technological innovation, information technology, all as the focus of cooperation to promote the China – Latin American industry docking.

② "3 x 3" model is the new model of China – Latin American production capacity cooperation proposed by Premier Li Keqiang in the speech of the China – Cuba Business and Industry Summit, namely, building the three major channels of logistics, electricity and information; implementing the interaction between enterprises, society and government; and building three financing channels of funds, credit, insurance, .

③ The reasonableness of this hypothesis is that in 2014, when President Xi Jinping visited Latin America, he said that China' s direct investment in Latin America will reach US $ 250 billion over the next 10 years.

of investors is rather dampened. Since 2015, Latin America has been facing an economic downturn. Major investment destinations like Brazil, Venezuela and other key countries underwent "negative growth, high inflation, and high unemployment". Enterprises are facing difficulties in their business operation and further investment might be suppressed.

The second factor is the business environment. In terms of business convenience, productivity cultivation and industry infrastructure, the global ranking of Latin America is poor, and the bottleneck factors are mainly reflected in the high tax standard, poor financing availability, limited government governance, inadequate supply of facilities, imperfect labor market and lack of industrial cooperation and supporting etc. All these factors may curb the enthusiasm of external investors.

Under the pressure listed above, the Chinese enterprises still face hindering factors to enter the Latin American market, which brings fluctuation towards the annual investment volume from China to Latin America in recent years. To a certain extent, this will affect the realization of investment objectives between the two sides.

Fifth, non – diplomatic factors are sensitive.

At present, there are 24 countries that have not established diplomatic relations with China, while Latin America accounts for 12. In the process of the overall cooperation with Latin America, China should be careful in dealing with non – diplomatic factors. First of all, communication and coordination will be difficult when it comes to non – diplomatic relations. The Community of Latin American and Caribbean States is composed of 33 independent countries in Latin America and the Caribbean. The "four carriages" (current rotating presidency, former rotating presidency, the next rotating presidency – elect and the CARICOM representative) can help with coordination and cooperation between China and Latin America, but the efficiency of the mechanism will be challenged when the non – diplomatic relations are involved in the "four carriages". Theoretically it is possible that three non – diplomatic countries could participate in the mechanism at the same time.

Therefore, early coordination and policy flexibility between the two sides become important to avoid the negative impact of non – diplomatic factors on the communication and convenience of the overall cooperation between the two sides. Secondly, the overall cooperation between China and Latin America, which includes non – diplomatic relations, may lead to a chain reaction of relations between the two sides of the Taiwan Strait. In particular, when cross – strait relations are tightened, the influence of non – diplomatic relations on the overall China – Latin America cooperation will be greater than ever. From this point of view, "non – diplomatic relations", "Taiwan factor" inevitably become two important variables in the medium and short term for the overall cooperation between the two sides.

3. Suggestions for General Policy – making Regarding the Overall Cooperation between China and Latin America

The overall cooperation between China and Latin America has a lot of driving forces, yet it is also faced with many challenges in reality which are difficult to avoid (some of them are even beyond our control). After the overall cooperation between China and Latin America has entered an institutionalized track of operation, policy makers from both sides have to make an objective assessment of the opportunities and challenges of cooperation between China and Latin America. They also have to conduct scientific analysis upon the contents and approaches of the overall cooperation so as to safeguard effectiveness and sustainability of the overall cooperation between China and Latin America.

China – Latin America's overall cooperation focuses on long – term and institutional arrangements. The development and implementation of the cooperation need to be conducted in a step – by – step manner and be gradually deepened. We have to strike a balance among short, medium and long – term goals and, in particular avoid blind and unrealistic goals. From the medium – short term perspective, our suggestions for the policy making of the overall cooperation between China and Latin America are as follows:

First, China should act as a major initiator and contributor to the overall cooperation so as to yield early harvest.

At the current stage, there are still disagreements from the two sides and within Latin American countries regarding the demands for and pursuit in the overall cooperation between China and Latin America. In particular, the counterpart of the Chinese government i.e. the Community of Latin American and Caribbean States is not a political entity. It is only a political agreement for regional integration reached by Latin American countries. It has yet not established a permanent secretariat. Therefore no substantial and binding resolution would be made and there were many restrictions on the implementation of the resolution.

Therefore, while the Community of Latin American and Caribbean States could not take the lead in pushing forward the overall cooperation between the two sides, China should, at this stage, take more initiatives in this regard and shoulder more responsibility correspondingly. By doing this, we will help to yield early harvest and stage results as soon as possible, enhance the centripetal force of this mechanism, and lay the foundation for its sustainable development.

To this end, based on the development needs from both sides, China should, under the guidance of the open – minded concept in the "13th Five – Year Plan", link the current "the Belt and Road Initiative" and other important strategic proposals and act as the major provider of public goods in the overall cooperation between China and Latin America. China needs to help to build the connectivity within Latin America, eliminate the constraints from infrastructure on regional integration, enhance the inner cohesion of the Community of Latin American and Caribbean States, and promote its symmetry status with China in the overall cooperation.

Second, China should place equal emphasis on trade, investment and finance as coordinated drivers for achieving trade goals between China and Latin America.

Economic and trade cooperation is both the foundation and driver of the overall cooperation. It is also the most frequently mentioned aspect in the "Chin – Latin America Cooperation Plan" published in 2015. Over the next 10 years, the two sides established our economic and trade cooperation goals such as "500 billion USD of trade and at least 250 billion USD of direct investment". This goal is not only one of the important early gains set by the overall cooperation mechanism, but also the cornerstone of the future direction of this mechanism it is also the top priority to deepen of the policy willingness and build mutual confidence from the two sides.

In the medium and short term, due to the economic downturn of Latin America, the realization of economic and trade cooperation is also influencing Latin America in calculating the economic benefits on the overall cooperation between the two sides. In order to better achieve this goal, China proposed to build a “1 +3 +6” new framework of cooperation and provides a new “3 × 3” path for energy capacity cooperation between China and Latin America. Based on the ideas above, China’s economic and trade cooperation model should gradually shift from simply relying on trade into a diversified model of trade, investment and financial cooperation.

In the days to come, we’ve got countless things to do. In trade, we should promote the dual marginal expansion of both import and export; overcome the decline in commodity prices and its negative impact on trade so as to meet the common needs of industrial upgrading and transformation from both sides and to promote a sound upgrade of China – Latin American trade.

In the area of investment, we should increase investment in manufacturing industry and infrastructure construction areas on the basis of traditional energy resources, infrastructure and agricultural cooperation so as to make substantial progress in cooperation between China and Latin America. Those measures could also make investment the new growth point in China – Latin American economic and trade cooperation.

In terms of finance, we should make full use of the overall cooperation platform between China and Latin America, and give full play to projects such as the China – Latin American Capacity Cooperation Investment Fund, China – Latin American Cooperative Fund etc. We also have too strengthen our cooperation such as local currency settlement, joint financing so as to better meet the need to promote the trade between China and Latin America and to upgrade bilateral investment. These measures can also help to address China’s demand to internationalize the RMB and Latin America’s need to stabilize it financial industry. What’s more, these approaches can provide a solid foundation for the two sides to better cooperate with each other in the global monetary system reform.

On the whole, a diversified model of trade and economic cooperation between China and Latin America is the only way to realize the 10–year goal agreed by the two sides and the must – go path to promote the deepening of economic and trade cooperation.

Third, we should strengthen cultural exchanges and people to people communication for better mutual perception and understanding.

Compared with the rapid growth of economic and trade cooperation, China and Latin America lack mutual recognition and political trust. In particular, we have to strengthen the people – to – people exchange which is vital for medium and short term sustainability. China and Latin America should and boost people to people exchange through multiple channels so as to strengthen mutual recognition and understanding. We can therefore consolidate the basis of the overall cooperation between China and Latin America.

Based on the status quo of cultural exchange and people – to – people communication between the two sides, our suggestions are as follows:

(1) Strengthen the "window – like" role of Confucius Institutes. As an important medium for the exchanges of education, Confucius Institute can consider enriching the content of its daily teaching by integrating China's national conditions into the language courses, thus change the Confucius Institute's role from "platform of promoting the Chinese language "to "window for the popularization of China's national conditions".

(2) Achieve institutionalization of the dialogue mechanisms between think tanks from both sides. At present, there are mainly two dialogue mechanisms in this aspect: one is the "China – Latin America Think Tank Exchange Forum" jointly established by the China International Research Foundation and the Chinese People's Institute of Foreign Affairs in 2010. So far, this forum has been held only twice. The other dialogue mechanism is the "China – Latin American Academic High – Level Forum" established in 2012 and jointly run by the Chinese Academy of Social Sciences Magazine, the Institute of Latin American Studies of

CASS, as well as the "Network of China Research "from major Latin American countries. Since 2012, the forum has been held on each side every other year for a total of four times.

We present two pieces of suggestions for the next step: we can integrate the two mechanisms into one and establish a think tank dialogue that covers broader areas, or we can maintain the two mechanisms with parallel independence but better implement each forum with favorable policy input. In addition, the think tanks from both sides can strengthen their joint research and provide targeted intellectual support for the overall cooperation.

(3) Strengthen the interaction between think tanks, government and enterprises. The current China – Latin America think tank exchange is facing financial shortages as its major difficulty. Think tanks (especially on the Chinese side) should strengthen their interaction with government, enterprises and international organizations. They can obtain more financial support through various approaches including both institutional cooperation and specialized agreements.

(4) Strengthen the "bridge" role of both Chinese and Chinese exporters. With more frequent exchanges between China and Latin America, the number of expatriates (especially Chinese expatriates in Latin America) will further increase. This group has a more objective understanding of the national conditions of China and Latin American countries as well as the current situation of China – Latin American relations. They are even directly or indirectly participating in the decision – making process of the host country, thus its importance should be taken seriously.

In this aspect, we should, on the one hand, improve our service for overseas Chinese, strengthen the consular protection, and promote the mutual recognition through diaspora groups. On the other hand, we will strengthen the communication and interaction with the Latin American Chinese organizations on our own territory. Although the current size of the Latin American Chinese in China is limited, most of them are consular officials, business representatives, and international students, all with comparatively objective and positive understanding of our country. In short, this importance cannot be underestimated.

(5) Strengthen the exchange and communication between

local governments from the two sides. Thanks to the support and encouragement of the National Association for Friendship with Foreign Countries, establishing pairs of sisterly cities has become the main platform for cooperation between China and the Latin American countries at the local government level. Since the establishment of the first pair of sister cities (Beijing and Lima in 1983), 151 pairs of sister cities/provinces have been formed between in China and 95 cities and 56 provinces in Latin America.① Since 2000 in particular, this number reached 110. At the local government level, there is huge space for deepening exchanges between China and Latin America, and its role can be further strengthened. Overall, the exchange of international students and think tanks can be set as priorities in the medium and short term people to people exchange.

Fourth, we have to better coordinate the existing bilateral and multilateral cooperation mechanisms and further establish a network of multi – channel cooperation mechanisms.

Although the two sides launched a mechanism for overall dialogue and cooperation, but the core content is still based on bilateral relations between China and Latin American countries as well as the relations between China and Latin American regional organizations and sub – regional organizations. Especially in the early years of the overall cooperation mechanism of China and Latin America, those two types of relations mentioned above will act as the pillars to support this young mechanism.

In addition, the "China – Latin America Forum" is an overall cooperation mechanism surpassing the bilateral relations. Its agenda and approach are negotiated and decided through a number of participating countries, which is different from the "complementary advantages" in bilateral cooperation. In such a framework of overall cooperation, some participating countries may have direct competition in certain areas or on some specific cooperation projects. Those potential conflicts should, to

① China International Friendship City Federation http://www.cifca.org.cn/Web/WordGuanXiBiao.aspx(date of research March 16th 2015).

some extent, be properly handled through bilateral consultation.

Therefore, we have to promote the the overall cooperation mechanism of China and Latin America through bilateral coordination with key countries. In the other way around, it is also necessary to fully utilize bilateral channels to solve unavoidable conflict of interests in the process of overall cooperation between the two sides. We must not let the overall cooperation be hampered by individual cases of competition. In addition, through bilateral channels, China can also coordinate differences of the Latin American countries in their position and interests so that the overall cooperation between China and Latin America will be as "focused" as possible.

It is also important to note that as China – Latin America's overall cooperation is based on the integration of Latin America and the Caribbean, China can use established dialogue mechanisms (such as the establishment of the dialogue mechanism with the Rio Group in 1990, with the MERCOSUR in 1997, with the Andean Community in 1999 etc.) to support regional integration projects including the Latin American Community, the Common Market of the South, the Andean Community, the Caribbean Community, the Rio Group, the Association of South American Nations, the Bavarian Union, Pacific Alliance and all others.

In doing so, we can promote a stable development of regional integration in Latin America and, on the other hand, can develop reasonable and meticulous regional cooperation arrangements based on the characteristics of this sub – region so as to achieve the balance and synergy between small and large, generalization and individuality.

Report Two

Current Situation and Perspectives on the Economic and Trade Relations and Production Capacity Cooperation between China and Latin America and the Caribbean

Yue Yunxia amd Wang Fei

Currently, world economy remains sluggish, with geopolitical conflicts on the rise. The "Brexit" is affecting the Europe profoundly, and the election of Donald Trump as U.S. president adds to the uncertainty of world's politics and economy. While at the same time, emerging markets are making more contributions to the global development, as South – South cooperation has become a major force in improving global economic governance. Asia and Latin America and the Caribbean (hereinafter referred to as "Latin America") are two regions where emerging economies are concentrated, and the cooperation between them is remarkable. In particular, the third visit of President Xi Jinping in November, 2016 and the timely release of China's Policy Paper on Latin America and the Caribbean not only opened a starting point in the community of shared destiny between China and Latin America, but also made a top – level design for promoting comprehensive and cooperative partnership. In the new context, cooperation between the two sides, especially production capacity cooperation will face brand new strategic opportunities.

1. Economic Situation in Latin America and the Caribbean: 2015—2016

According to *2016 Preliminary Overview of the Economies of Latin America and the Caribbean*[①] issued by Comisión Económica para América Latina y el Caribe (hereinafter referred to as CEPAL), regional economy of Latin America in 2015 contracted by 0.5%, the first time since 2009, prolonging the economic growth slowdown that had begun in 2011. In 2016, the GDP of Latin America contracted by 1.1%, the first drop of regional economy for two consecutive years since the 1980s (see Table 1). At the same time, the inflation reached 16.5% in 2016, a rise of 7.1 percentage points on the 2014 rate of 9.4%. The inflation rate in 2015 was the highest since that of 1996 when the inflation rate was as high as 18%. The rise of inflation was heavily influenced by the Bolivarian Republic of Venezuela, whose inflation rate was 180.9%.[②] Therefore, economy in Latin America and the Caribbean has been generally sluggish in the past two years.

Table 1:
Latin America and the Caribbean: main economic indicators during 2012–2016

	2012	2013	2014	2015	2016
		Annual growth rates			
GDP	2.8	2.9	0.9	–0.5	–1.1
Per capita GDP	1.7	1.7	–0.2	–1.6	–2.2
CPI	4.9	5.0	6.3	7.9	…
		Percentages			
Urban open unemployment	7.4	7.2	7.0	7.4	9.0
Total gross external debt/GDP	28.4	30.2	32.6	34.9	36.4

① Statistics in this part come from the latest report of CEPAL unless specifically noted. See also CEPAL, 2016 Preliminary Overview of the Economies of Latin America and the Caribbean, 2016.

② Even with the exception of Venezuela, the inflation rate in Latin America and the Caribbean rose from 6.3% in 2014 to 7.9% in 2015.

(Contd.)

	2012	2013	2014	2015	2016
Total gross external debt/ Exports of goods and services	97	103	113	133	150
Millions of dollars					
Current account balance	–132946	–158757	–187309	–182356	–106048
Exports of goods	1116309	1098679	1083709	925306	865918
Imports of goods	1076040	1096310	1102198	984375	774115
Services trade balance	–72815	–72306	–73438	–51013	–37687
Income balance	–158172	–146899	–157035	–136214	–124908
Net current transfers	62073	62318	65745	67878	71776
Capital and financial balance	186226	163719	219038	104825	125729
Net FDI	149269	142677	143456	129292	576
Other capital movements	36957	21042	75581	–24468	125153
International reserves	835735	830018	857438	811762	829202
Percentages of GDP					
Overall fiscal balance	–1.9	–2.6	–2.8	–3.0	–3.0
Primary fiscal balance	–0.2	–0.9	–1.0	–0.9	–0.8
Central – government public debt	30.5	32.3	33.6	36.5	37.9

Source: CEPAL, 2016 Preliminary Overview of the Economies of Latin America and the Caribbean, 2016, Table A–1.

However, regional experience indicates that the overall situation often conceals the heterogeneity of sub regions and countries. Owing to low energy prices, upturn of U.S. demand and inflows of overseas remittance, as well as inflation trends that allow for a degree of policy space for stimulating domestic aggregate demand, Central America maintained relatively robust growth. Similarly, Mexico's economy grew by 2% in 2016 because of the U.S. economic recovery. By contrast, the southern states were faced with a major deterioration in their terms of trade conditions, weaker external aggregate demand (from China and intraregional partners) and a significant narrowing of their space to maneuver in terms of adopting demand – stimulus policies due to high inflation and dependence on primary commodity export, so the economy decreased by 2.4%, worse than 2009, when the GDP decreased by 0.2%. Besides, economy in the Caribbean region also decreased 1.7% because of the slower growth of service industries, and the serious economic deterioration of nations which depend on primary products export heavily. ①

Apart from the stagflation, the macro economy and economic policies in Latin America have the following features.

First of all, driving force of economic growth has lost its economic vitality. Domestic demand shrank by 1.6% in 2015, resulted from the declines in both final consumption (–0.2%) and gross capital formation (–6.5%). Conversely, owing both to growth in exports and to a decline in imports, net exports rose significantly and became the main contributor to economic growth. Besides, the contribution of private consumption has turned negative in the first quarter of 2015, therefore it ceased to underpin aggregate demand. Due to the shrinking in architecture industry and machinery and equipment industry, gross fixed capital began to decline since the second quarter of 2014. Private consumption and fixed capital investment that drove the economic growth have lost vitality. From the supply side, service industry was the only positive contributor to the development since the second quarter of 2014, with the negative or zero contributions from the first and second industries. However, since the third quarter of 2015, all of the three industries began to contribute negatively to regional development.

Second, the fall in primary commodity prices has led to heterogeneity of terms of trade in sub – regions. According to the export commodity price index compiled by CEPAL, prices fell by 29% on average in 2015, with the following variations by sector: prices for energy products were down by 42%, metals and minerals by 23% and agricultural products by 16%. The impact of this trend in prices on the terms of trade is uneven and depends on the weight of different commodities in the export and import basket of each country. The countries hardest hit were those whose exports are concentrated mainly in petroleum and natural gas, as their terms of trade fell by 30%. They were followed by countries

① Caribbean countries that are relied on primary products include Guyana, Suriname and Trinidad and Tobago, the rest of the Caribbean countries are specialized in the service industry.

whose main exports are minerals and metals and agro – industrial products, whose terms of trade fell by 5% and 3% respectively. These countries benefited to some extent from the lower oil prices. Although manufactured goods for the United States market account for a large share of its exports, Mexico is a net exporter of energy products –mainly crude oil – and was thus hit sharply by the sharp fall in prices in this sector in 2015, leading to a 5% drop in its terms of trade. By contrast, Central American countries and the Caribbean countries (excluding Trinidad and Tobago) benefited from the change in prices, as they are net importers of food and energy products, and their terms of trade improved by 6% and 1% respectively.(see figure 1) These trends are expected to continue in 2016.

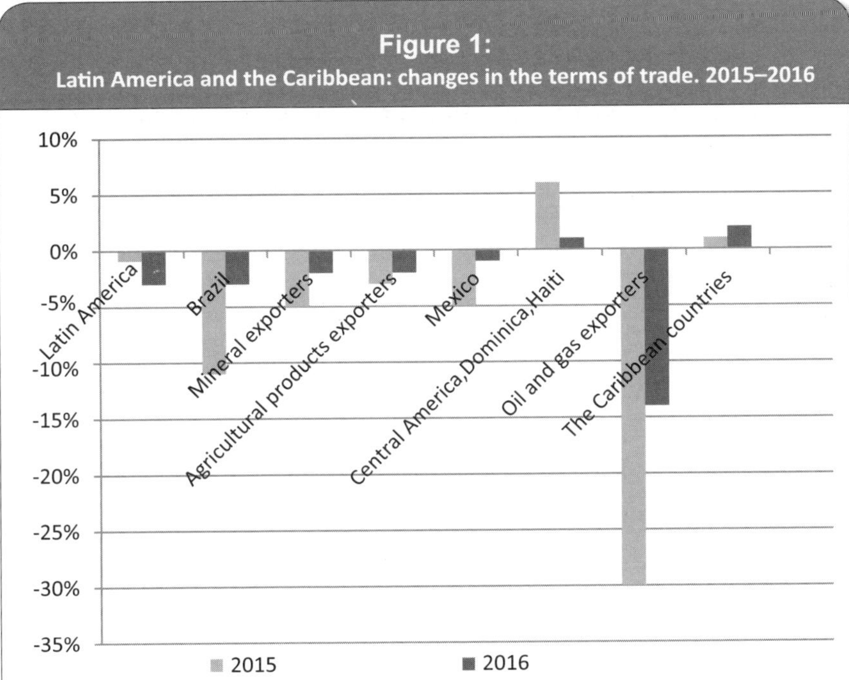

Figure 1:
Latin America and the Caribbean: changes in the terms of trade. 2015–2016

Note: Mining commodities exporters include Chile and Peru; agro – industrial commodities exporters are Argentina, Paraguay and Uruguay; petroleum and natural gas exporters are Bolivarian Republic of Venezuela, Colombia, Ecuador, Pluri – national State of Bolivia and Trinidad and Tobago; the Caribbean countries don't include Trinidad and Tobago.

Source: CEPAL, 2016 Economic Survey of Latin America and the Caribbean: The 2030 Agenda for Sustainable Development and the challenges of financing for development, July 26, 2016.

Third, both current account and fiscal account showed deficits. On the regional front, the deficit on current account has been long existed, and its proportion in GDP increased significantly. This demonstrates Latin America s high – level of dependence on external capital and its venerability in face of potential balance – of – payments crisis. On the central government front, primary fiscal deficit accounted for 0.8% of GDP in 2016, and overall deficit (including public debt interest payment) 3% (see Table 1), on the verge of the warning line of 3% made by the international community. Although central governments' public debt accounted for 37.9% of GDP in 2016, which is at a relatively low level, this couldn't conceal the high debt load rate in the Caribbean region, Brazil and Argentina. The deficits in both accounts have threatened debt governance and international balance of payments, shaking confidence of investors in the economic prospects in Latin America and the Caribbean.

Fourth, the risks of sovereign debt and currency volatility shall not be neglected. Measured by the Emerging Market Bond Index Global (EMBIG), the risks in Latin America increased markedly in 2015, linked in part to the increased volatility in global financial market, and to specific national factors in some countries that pushed up the regional index. In January 2016, EMBIG reached 677 basis points, the highest level seen since 2009.In line with a less tense global financial market, this index dropped to 522 basis points, still higher than the 508 basis points of 2014. Currently the countries with high sovereign risk are Bolivarian Republic of Venezuela (2659 basis points), Ecuador (913 basis points), Argentina (496 basis points), the Dominican Republic (428 basis points) and Brazil (366 basis points). In 2015, currency depreciation in Latin America continued: the currencies of 16 countries in the region depreciated against the dollar in nominal terms, 9 of them by more than 10%, with Argentina by 52.8%, Brazil by 49% and Colombia by 33.6% respectively. It should be noted that the upturn of sovereign risks and currency volatility would lead to the outflow of capital, and finally impact internal financial system and real economy negatively.

Fifth, the weak labor market adversely affected the improvement of social conditions. The economic growth slowdown in Latin America did not manifest itself in higher unemployment (see Table 1) because although the employment rate did drop in the region as fewer wage –

paying jobs were created, an even larger contraction in the participation rate prevented this from being reflected in higher open unemployment. However, due to the continued macroeconomic deterioration, this trend altered in 2015, resulting in the region's open unemployment rate rising for the first time since 2009, from 7% in 2014 to 7.4%. Specifically, the further weakening of waged job creation and a slump of incomes forced many poor households to step up the search for earnings, which resulted in the expansion of own – account working and a concomitant deterioration in employment quality. Due to the continued economic decline in Latin America, the influx of job – seekers has been a factor in the significant increase the participation rate, which raised the urban open unemployment rate to 9%. This would not only reverse the improvement of weakening social inequality through income distribution system, but also weaken economic growth through consumption. Therefore, labor market can never be attached too much importance to as it is a bridge linking economic growth and social development.

Sixth, macroeconomic policies underwent double tests of "divergence" and "dilemma". Inflation patterns have shaped the various monetary and exchange rate policies in Latin America and the Caribbean: in the south, higher inflation has reduced the scope for policies to stimulate aggregate demand, while has widened it in the north. The central banks of South American countries that use interest rates as their main monetary policy instrument tend to raise their interest rate in order to cope with the rise in inflation. During 2015, Brazil, Chile, Colombia and Peru raised their monetary policy interest rate by 250, 50, 125, and 25 basis points respectively. However, monetary authorities of these countries are facing a dilemma in which the raise of rate may discourage investors, and expansionary monetary policies they have applied to stimulate aggregate demand may be undermining price stability. Meanwhile, in the economies of Central America and the Caribbean, lower inflationary pressures have allowed central banks to adopt monetary policies to stimulate lending demand and aggregate demand. Mexico was an exception to this trend in the northern part of the region. Mexico's central bank raised interest rate by 25 basis points in December 2015, and again by 50 basis points in February 2016. Factors such as the increase of the United States federal funds rate and the volatility of international financial markets weighed on its final decisions. During 2015–2016, countries in Latin America continued to implement macro – prudential regulation policies. In order to ease exchange rates volatility and strengthen the status in international currency reserves, a number of measures were taken, such as adopting currency swap scheme, restarting the flexible credit system of IMF for Colombia and Mexico, and being assured of the possession of resources from multilateral institutions. Argentina cancelled its monetary controls at the end of 2015; Bolivarian Republic of Venezuela and Bahamas altered their regulations on foreign exchange configuration mechanism; Bolivia, Costa Rico, Haiti and Peru began their efforts to de – dollarize their payment systems.

2. The Economic and Trade Relations between China and the Community of Latin American and Caribbean States Enter a New Stage of "the Two Ten – Year Goals"

As a core element and an important engine for this bilateral relationship, China and the Community of Latin American and Caribbean States have set a new goal that the bilateral trade and investment will approximately be doubled within ten years. "The two ten – year goals" has defined the medium – term and long – term targets which serve as the foundation for the result – oriented cooperation between the two sides. Its realization concerns the quality and progress of the overall cooperation and currently embraces good opportunities for development, but also confronts internal and external pressure and challenges. This needs the two sides to adjust themselves in a timely manner so as to meet the demands of development of the bilateral relations in this new phase.

2.1 The Definition and Significance of "the Two Ten – Year Goals"

At the beginning of this century, during the rapid development of bilateral relations, the expansion of economic and trade cooperation formed healthy interactions with high – level and people to people exchanges along with social interactions, which opened a new era of our friendly relationship. In order to promote comprehensive, in – depth and fast development of the practical cooperation, China has announced an initiative of building the new "1+3+6" framework for pragmatic cooperation and, published *the China – Latin American and the Caribbean Countries Cooperation Plan (2015–2019)* (hereafter referred to as "Plan") at the first ministerial meeting of the Forum of China and the Community of Latin American and Caribbean States in January 2015. Under this new framework, bilateral trade and investment serve as the main engine for mutual cooperation. The "Plan" has identified "the two ten – year goals" and clearly pointed out that "we will take joint efforts to promote two – way trade as well as balanced and mutually beneficial development in order to make our trade volume total $500 billion and the investment stock reach $250 billion and beyond".

"The two ten – year goals" about trade and investment is one of the few specific targets in the "Plan" and has set the direction for the two sides to continuously expand cooperation. It has been one of the important manifestations that joint cooperation could bring fruits very early, and thus has great significance for the steady development of the bilateral relationship. First, trade and investment are the driving forces for the new framework for pragmatic cooperation, while the realization of the two ten – year goals serves as the safeguard for smoothly advancing this mutual cooperation. Since 2013, Chinese leaders have provided a series of initiatives and proposals to speed up quality improvement and upgrading of the cooperation between China and Latin America. The new "1+3+6" framework for pragmatic cooperation and the new "3×3" model for capacity cooperation are the core content and the priority path respectively. Trade and investment are the focuses and specific methods for implementation of the above initiatives. "The two ten – year goals" set by quantitative indicators is the substantive content of the overall cooperation and also the focus of promoting bilateral relations as well as concerns the progress of cooperation between China and Latin America.

Second, "the two ten – year goals" has created great opportunities for both sides to enable healthy interactions and laid a foundation for win – win outcomes. Through recent 10 years of development, China and Latin America, which is interdependent, has initially built up the community of shared future. Under the pressure and difficulties brought about by economic slowdown facing both sides, "the two ten – year goals" is aimed at strengthening the bilateral cooperation. It helps China to realize scale effect of advanced capacity so as to balance economic structure and also benefits the Latin American and Caribbean countries to improve infrastructure so as to diversify its economic structure. Therefore, it has become an effective means to achieve win – win outcomes and a cornerstone for the overall cooperation. Meanwhile, in the age of China's new normal in economic development, the community of Latin American and Caribbean Countries will continue to be a supplier of resources, energy and intermediate products for China, a recipient of China's goods and capacity with competitive advantages, a practitioner of China's innovative technologies and standards and an important partner of China's overseas economic strategy. All these mentioned above are vital for China's key economic interests. China's trade and investment are the main means for it to realize economic interests in Latin America. "The two ten – year goals" could ensure a steady expansion of China's interests.

As a result, the successful accomplishment of "the two ten – year goals" marks a critical step for the two sides to conduct overall cooperation and will be of great significance for both to release structural and cyclical pressure as well as set a new example to conduct South – South cooperation.

2.2 Opportunities and Challenges Facing "the Two Ten – Year Goals"

In this context, China and Latin America are now experiencing economic transformations. "The two ten – year goals" has gained the conditions to seize the historical opportunities created by the development in both sides, yet still confront some realistic challenges.

2.2.1 Historical Opportunities

"The two ten – year goals" was initially designed for the rapid development of bilateral economic and trade cooperation and based on the historical opportunities created by a specific stage of the current development. From 2000 to 2012, the bilateral trade has remained an average annual growth of more than 30%, trade volume has increased by nearly 20–fold and investment also showed an accelerated growth in 2009. The ultra – high – speed development and the two economies' rapid growth are mutually supportive. Even though both sides have experienced varying degrees of economic slowdown since 2013, in the meantime both have entered a period featuring in – depth transformation and adjustment, which has generated a great many new opportunities, and laid a foundation for the realization of "the two ten – year goals".

China's economic transformation takes supply – side reform as its target and thereby this provides opportunities of commodity and capital for Latin America and the Caribbean. On the one hand, China's industrial upgrading and adjustment offers an incremental market for Latin America. At present, China's economic structure has shifted to the tertiary industry as its largest proportion and consumption has become the main driver of economic growth. The demand for commodity slowed down, but the demand for importing consumptive goods rose, and thus new opportunities have been created for Latin America to export its agricultural products and other goods with comparative advantage. On the other hand, China's transformation on capital flows could provide incremental investment for Latin America. China has been a net exporter of capital since 2014. In the field of direct investment, it has become the second largest investor to oversea destinations and Latin America has become China's second foreign investment destination. In the area of financial investment, China's lending to Latin America has totaled $94 billion, whereas the aggregate loan from the World Bank, CAF – Latin American Development Bank and the Inner – American Development Bank just summed up to $156 billion. Capital from China has met its deficiency of funds and has become an important safeguard for stabilizing its financial environment.

The economic transformation in Latin America is mainly driven by demand, which offers China opportunities to expand its market. In the near future, new demands in this region concentrate in three areas: first, the demand for investment in energy, road and other "hardware"; second, the demand for in communication, the Internet and other "software"; third, the demand for upgrading its industrial economy. These sectors have supplied China market opportunities to transfer its capacity with advantages. Based on such models as economic and trade cooperation zone, free trade zone, export processing zone and industrial park, China and Latin America share broad prospects for cooperation in clean energy, new building materials, petrochemical, automotive, steel, agricultural products, port logistics, information technology etc.

The early development of the bilateral cooperation was built on the natural and static complementarity of the two economic structures, while the current development creates possibilities to conduct dynamic complementarity. Adjustment, transformation and upgrading of the bilateral cooperation in economic and trade have stepped up since 2013, which fits well with the economic development of the current stage in both sides. Therefore, the basic conditions for realizing "the two ten – year goals" have been prepared well.

2.2.2 Realistic Challenges

While embracing historical opportunities, "the two ten – year goals" is also confronting challenges from the practical environment. In order to meet these two goals, from 2015 to 2024, the average annual growth of bilateral trade should reach 6.6. % and the bilateral investment stock should exceed 8.2%. According to the customs statistics, the growth of the bilateral investment stock has surpassed the necessary rate; nevertheless, the growth of the bilateral trade has been evidently marginal, just hitting 0.1% and 0.7% in 2013 and 2014 respectively, and even showed a year – on – year decline of 10.2% in 2015 and further shrank by 10.9% in the first ten month of 2016. Thus, the recent pressure on the cooperation mainly comes from the bilateral trade. To achieve these two goals needs the two sides to stimulate trade and steadily promote the investment environment. However, this faces multiple challenges.

First, constraints of the trade structure between China and Latin America. Through the ternary marginal decomposition of the product type, price and quality of the bilateral trade, it can be seen that the pressure on growth mainly derived from stagnation of quantity and the further concentration of exports style since 2012. In the meantime, China's export to this region stayed in the lower value – added range, implying China still took low price as its competitive advantage. This led to a degree of competition against the local manufacture which Latin America has currently endeavored to push forward so that the growth space has been limited. In the short– to medium– terms, due to the structural rigidness existing in the bilateral trade, the economic downturn in both economies and the sluggish global commodity prices will amplify pressure on the bilateral trade. Besides, the over – concentration of product structure will also limit the growth space of the bilateral trade. Only more in – depth upgrading and transformation of the bilateral trade structure can help the two sides create new growth points.

Second, constraints of the liberalization and facilitation of the bilateral trade and investment. In terms of openness, in the area of investment, some countries in this region still have restrictive regulations on the foreign investment access. In the field of trade, China and its major trade partners such as Brazil have high level of comprehensive trade restrictions, the same with the restrictions on trade in competitive sectors. In the matter of facilitation, both sides confront bottlenecks restricting economic and trade cooperation. In most countries of Latin America, overlong application period for visa, poor infrastructure and inefficient logistics as well as overt or covert cost on many things like tax still exist. These have constrained the development of bilateral cooperation. As for China, its supplementary policies and measures for enterprises to go global are lagging behind its due demand; some existing policies, such as mortgage policy and restrictions on business scope of the state – owned enterprises, lack flexibility. These have affected the bilateral cooperation as well. These areas of weakness have exerted a negative impact on the achievement of "the two ten – year goals", especially on the steady expansion of investment.

Third, uncertainties of business environment derived from the politics in Latin America. Changes of the political situation in major countries of this region were interwoven with international factors. Thus, the regional political ecology has become more complex. First, a trend of "right – leaning" has appeared in this region's politics. Regimes changes and political divergences will increase the uncertainties of investment and business environment. Second, the new "right – wing" government resorts to a "balanced foreign strategy" to strengthen relationship with the West. Therefore, the political dividend enjoyed by the bilateral economic and trade activities was impacted. Furthermore, the return of populism since the start of this century, influencing the political system, could easily split united groups and make governments short – sighted. This has posed a potential threat to the sustainability of policies and the stability of business environment. In addition, recently other major economies have expanded their resource investment in Latin America, and especially the United States has accelerated to get back to this region. The normalization of U.S.–Cuba diplomatic relationship and other landmark events have great impact on the political situation of this region. Moreover, black swan incidents throughout the world and changes in this region during this year will also further enlarge uncertainties caused by the external factors. These above changes will have an important impact on the overall cooperation and the uncertainties occurring in the bilateral economic and trade cooperation environment, and hence will increase the difficulties in realizing "the two ten – year goals".

Fourth, potential risks posed by Latin America's legal systems. The region gets middling global raking on the overall level of rule of law. Legislation in some areas surpasses the current situation and therefore poses high requirements for Chinese investments and operations in the region. Strict environmental protection laws of Latin America countries entail great uncertainty and slow approval for resources – related investments of China. In addition, as many countries in the region legislate to protect land rights of the aboriginal people and most of the resources that are yet to be explored are found in Indian Reservation Areas, issues arising from the aboriginal community and conflicts between protection of the aboriginal culture and economical development as well as resources exploration pose one of the most prominent risks for investments by resources companies. On the front of labor protection, trade unions represent a powerful force and minimum wage laws are most common in Latin America where high level of social security and sclerotic and fragmented labor market coexist. All these factors increase the risks and difficulties of employment. The aforementioned legal circumstances result in invisible constraints and increase risks for Chinese companies' operations in the region.

Fifth, systemic risks caused by social issues in Latin America. Latin America are among the regions where social issues are most prominent. First, the fruits of economic development are not fairly shared by all, resulting in an ever – widening gap between the rich and the poor, insufficient savings ratio and inadequate consumption. Second, Latin America has poor public security. The crime rate in the region is well above world average and drug – related crimes are epidemic. In addition, social movements have frequented over the years. Strikes, labor disputes and movements of the Indians, landless peasants and laid – off workers break out from time to time, impacting businesses' production and operation. As bilateral economic and trade cooperation deepens, social issues constrains market growth and deteriorate investment environment, thus detrimental to the fulfilling the two ten – year goals.

2.2.3 Thinking on Ways to Fulfill the Two Ten – Year Goals

The two ten – year goals of bilateral trade and investment demonstrate the political willingness of both parties to expand the breadth and depth of cooperation. There exist both favorable conditions and difficulties and challenges for fulfilling the goals, which requires both parties to stay committed to the targets that must be met and make adjustments when situations change.

First, we should stick to the direction towards greater trade and investment between the two sides and hedge against short – term fluctuations with long – term goals. Local markets of Latin America have traditionally been subject to cyclical volatilities, to which the US and European countries with high market share respond with the strategy of "time for space". The two ten – year goals are in the interests of both parties and points out direction for bilateral cooperation in the future. As a new comer in Latin American and the Caribbean market, China could draw experience from the US and EU countries like Spain, and stay cool – headed in response to temporary fluctuations for the interests for long – term operations.

Second, we should continue to advance political ties to create favorable conditions for economic and trade cooperation. In response to the recent changes in politics of the region, China should put its national interests first, maintain bilateral friendship and stay out of the internal disputes of countries in the region. China should take a long – term perspective, explore multiple ways of cooperation and maintain good communication with both left wing and right wing parties. In order to be prepared against project risks brought by change of government, China should make its policies towards the region more flexible and act in the interests of bilateral cooperation to adjust its projects when necessary. Flexibility of political cooperation helps ensure stability of economic and trade cooperation and create conditions for the fulfillment of the two ten – year's goals.

Third, we should promote innovation on multiple fronts to overcome bottlenecks to economic and trade cooperation. Against downturn in bilateral trade and uncertainties of investment environment, the key to meeting the two goals is to find new growth points and to offset or even eliminate uncertainties by institutional innovations. As for institutional innovations, both parties should enhance institutional building for bilateral economic and trade cooperation, lower tariff and non – tariff barriers, facilitate trade and investment, and expand the scope of free trade agreement to push forward bilateral economic and trade relations towards mutual benefit. To innovate the structure of bilateral trade, China could import more competitive agricultural products from the region and export more products of higher added value so as to contribute to the domestic supply side structural reform and the leap forward from "made in China" to "invented in China". For institutional innovation from within China, the Chinese government should streamline its administration and change the regulations that have far lagged behind. In the past, China's cooperation with the region has been led by the government with the state owned enterprises acting as pioneers. This pattern should be changed so that market – oriented cooperation and private businesses could go hand in hand with government – led collaboration and the state owned enterprises.

Fourth, we should uphold win – win cooperation for all parties to promote inclusive development of the region. Win – win cooperation is the essence of China's relations with Latin American and the Caribbean countries. As the newcomer to the market, China can only prevent conflicts and bring benefits to all parties by "growing the pie" of the market. For that end, China needs to follow its second policy paper on Latin America, and "carry out trilateral development cooperation in Latin American and Caribbean countries with relevant countries outside the region and international organizations" to achieve win – win results for all. China also needs to seize the opportunities arising from global industrial restructuring and enter Latin America market by drawing the strengths from EU countries, in particular Spain and Portugal whose presences have been well established in the region. This is a smart way to do less for more.

Fifth, we should have a deeper understanding of the differences between China's legal system and that of the region at large so as to break the cultural and legal bottlenecks. Faced with complex legal systems in

Latin America, China should attach greater importance to preliminary research on the legal environment and the training of law professionals. Moreover, China should strictly abide by the laws and regulations of the hosting country, in particular laws on labor, taxation, environmental protection and protection of indigenous rights, and actively assume social responsibilities. Should legal disputes arise, China should firstly resort to international commerce arbitration that is well recognized by countries in this region for more just legal treatment.

3. Analysis and Prospects of Production Capacity Cooperation between China and Latin America

Relationship between China and Latin America has been centered into economic and trade cooperation, whose highlight has been production capacity cooperation. After the leap – forward development since the beginning of this century, economic and trade cooperation between China and Latin America is transforming from the simple trade – oriented cooperation to complete cooperation whose core is production capacity cooperation. With demands and favorable conditions for the promotion of production capacity cooperation, China and Latin America, on the basis of current cooperation models, are in a good position to explore more ways for cooperation and better synergize the production capacity in key industries.

3.1 Conditions and Demands of Production Capacity Cooperation between China and Latin America

3.1.1 Conditions for Production Capacity Cooperation between China and Latin America

(1) The Good Foundation in Economy and Trade Indicates Huge Potential for Production Capacity Cooperation

At present, China is the second largest trading partner of Latin America and the third largest investor in this region. Bilateral trade volume has increased from 12.6 billion dollars in 2000 to 263.6 billion dollars in 2014, an increase of 20 fold. In 2015, China and Latin America made a commitment to work hard and raise the trade volume to 500 billion dollars in 10 years, with bilateral investment stock exceeding 250 billion dollars. With the ever closer trade ties, China and Latin America embarked on a new era where bilateral cooperation and overall cooperation co – exist and reinforce each other.

For a long period, trade has been the pillar of economic and trade cooperation between China and Latin America, outracing investment cooperation. With the trade potential being unleashed, the space for both sides to expand export is limited, while investment cooperation has entered a new era. Among the major countries in Latin America, China's investment potential indices are all positive and outnumber trade potential indices, indicating huge potential for production capacity cooperation between China and Latin America (see Figure 2). The two sides need to attach importance on international production capacity cooperation as it is a new growth point of future economic and trade cooperation. Cooperation on production capacity will not only implement the overall cooperation vision between China and Latin America, but also will coordinate the development strategies by leveraging advantages of both sides, so as to achieve win – win situation and boost world economic recovery.

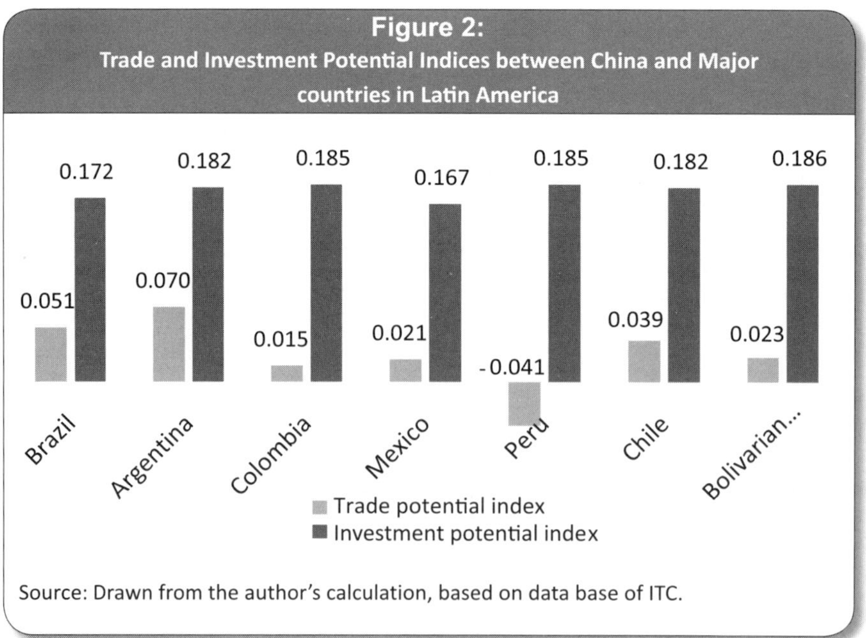

(2) Institutional Conditions

In recent years, Chinese government has vigorously developed "going out" strategy and encourages Chinese enterprises to invest abroad. Since the 21st century, Chinese government further deepened its reform, especially after the release of Decision of the State Council on Reforming the Investment System; it reformed project approval system, giving enterprises greater independence in making investment decisions. Consequently, the approval system that was based on record – filing and supplemented by review and approval was established. According to the Directory of Government – Approved Investment Projects (2014), Chinese government has theoretically eased admittance restrictions on foreign investment, with the exception of some sensitive areas and sensitive industries. Documents such as Measures for the Administration of Outbound Investment issued by Ministry of Commerce, and Measures for the Administration of Confirmation and Recordation of Overseas Investment Project (2014) promulgated by State Development & Reform Commission further facilitated outbound investment and cooperation for Chinese enterprises. Opinions of the State Council on Promoting the Production Capacity Cooperation and Equipment Manufacturing promulgated in 2015 systematically proposed targets in 12 key fields such as steel, non – ferrous metals, building materials, railway, electricity, textile, automobile, communications, engineering machinery, aerospace, ship and marine engineering, comprehensively deploying work to strengthen coordination and guidance, and improving foreign cooperation mechanism by reforming the management system. From May 18 to 26, 2015, during his visit in Brazil, Colombia, Peru and Chile, Premier Li Keqiang once again stressed the importance of production capacity cooperation. On September 1, the People's Bank of China, the State Administration of Foreign Exchanges, and the China Development Bank jointly established China – Latin American Production Capacity Cooperation Investment Fund, and the initial investment that reached 10 billion dollars were mainly invested in major medium – and long – term projects in areas such as serve industry, new technology, agriculture, new energy and infrastructure.

In 2015, China and Brazil signed 35 concrete cooperation agreements, covering areas such as bilateral production capacity, infrastructure, finance, aviation and agriculture, with total trade volume exceeding 27 billion dollars; China and Colombia signed 12 bilateral cooperation agreements in such areas as infrastructure, production capacity, assistance, culture and education; China announced with Peru that China was ready to participate in railway transportation programs such as the Twin Ocean Railroad Connection project, and to promote technical transfer alongside cooperation on equipment, so as to promote the connectivity of Latin America; China and Chile also signed agreements to step up cooperation in finance, production capacity and equipment industry. These efforts have provided a favorable institutional environment for China – Latin American cooperation on production capacity.

(3) China's Strength in Equipment Manufacturing and Infrastructure Construction

After years of rapid development, China's equipment manufacturing now features wide range, high technology and complete industry system, and its industrial scale has been the largest in the world for 5 consecutive years. China's machine tools output accounts for 38% of the world, shipbuilding completion 41%, and power generation equipment output 60%. China's high – speed railway outraces that of the other countries in the world. Thanks to decades of inbound investment and independent development, China has reached world – class levels in such areas as high – speed railway, hydroelectric power and infrastructure, with more than 200 kinds of products ranking the first in the world. China's products, with telecommunications equipment as the representative, are highly competitive and cost – effective; Chinese capital, equipment and technology enjoy greater popularity among countries, especially developing countries. Meanwhile, China's serious overcapacity problems in steel, cement, electrolytic aluminum, flat glass, ship and photovoltaic industries can be resolved by international production capacity cooperation, which will not only yield profits, thus promoting internal economic development, but also provide a platform for Chinese enterprises to participate in international competition, upgrade technology, improve quality and service, and strengthen overall quality and core competitiveness, so as to promote the transformation and upgrading of manufacturing and economic restructuring.

In 2014, the value of China's equipment manufacturing export reached 2.1 trillion Yuan, and large – sized complete sets of equipment export 110 billion dollars. Fruitful results have been generated in production capacity cooperation between China and Latin American and the Caribbean. China outraces most countries in the region in terms of price, quality, and technology, forming a gradient difference in technology, so it is able to gain market share in the region by introducing related technology and equipment here.

From January to April in 2015, the turnover of Chinese foreign contracted projects reached 41.85 billion US dollars, a 15% year – on – year increase; the value of newly signed contracts was 56.76 billion, a 29.6% increase over the previous year. As Chinese enterprises are quite competitive in such areas as housing construction, transportation infrastructure, communications, industrial manufacturing and petrochemical, newly signed contracts value grew rapidly, which ensures the sustainable development of Chinese overseas projects. Even in short duration, Chinese engineering contractors are able to complete a variety of large – scale infrastructure projects, including the highest railway, the largest dam, the tallest building and all kinds of highway and railway projects that were completed in complex geological conditions. The progress that Chinese enterprises have made in various fields demonstrates that they are advanced in the use of professional construction equipment, the project management experience of the staff, their ability to fulfill diversified demand and to better help countries in this region to improve their infrastructure.

3.1.2. Demands of Production Capacity Cooperation between China and Latin America

(1) Demands of Developing and Upgrading Industries

External and internal factors jointly contribute to the sluggish economic development in Latin America. On the one hand, the lackluster world economy has been compounded by the economic slowdown of emerging markets including China. In this context, overseas demand of resources, energy and commodities contracted, with prices being pulled down. On the other hand, with the shortage of growth points and the driving force of innovation, the development pattern of Latin America needs to be improved.

Due to high reliance on the rich resources, the economic structure and development pattern Latin America as a whole has contributed to the fact that the region depend too much on foreign investment. Now with the sluggish world economy, it's no doubt that Latin American and the Caribbean economy abound with problems. Problems of its economic structure such as low level of overall savings, weak capacity of companies' overseas investment, high tax costs and unbalanced industrial structure. These will by no means be solved in a short period of time. But if no large – scale structural reform is taken, the level of economic development will remain low in the future.

As China readjusts and upgrades its industrial structure in the "new norm", Latin America needs to restructure its industries to promote competitiveness and status in global industrial value chain. The acceleration of global industrial structure readjustment and infrastructure construction, especially the vigorous promotion of industrialization in developing countries has created important opportunities and favorable environment for China to speed up international cooperation on production capacity and equipment manufacturing. It is a global trend to conduct international production capacity cooperation and promote industrialization and re – industrialization through investing in real economy. [①] Against this backdrop, international production capacity cooperation will optimize and upgrade cooperation between China and Latin America, bringing new growth points for world economy and national development. [②]

(2) Demands of Optimizing Trading Structure

Despite of high level of resources and energy complementarity between China and Latin America, the sustainable economic and trade cooperation couldn't last for long with the current structure. With China's economic slowdown, readjustment of economic structure and the slump of global commodities, traditional trade relation between the two sides that relies heavily on resources, energy and commodities face mounting challenges.

① 梁敏：《"产能合作"开启中拉新里程》，《上海证券报》2015年5月27日。
② 李克强：《推动中巴合作升级 引领中拉共同发展》，《人民日报》2015年5月21日。

Both China and Latin America face challenges in transforming and upgrading economy. In order to support economic upgrading, both sides need to strengthen production capacity cooperation: Latin America cannot rest easy as being the "global supplier" of primary goods, and China cannot always be the "world factory" of cheap products; both sides need to upgrade and readjust industries, as the traditional trade structure that centered on general industrial consumer goods exchange and mineral – based products is not sustainable.

To realize the sustainable development of economic and trade relations between China and Latin America, it is necessary to transform economic and trade structure, diversify exports to China and increase the added value of Latin American and the Caribbean exports. Production capacity cooperation, which will readjust trade structure and better synergize industries, is the key to and method of bilateral trade to get out of the mire. China's export of surplus production capacity to Lain America and the Caribbean will inject impetus to industrial development and unleash new trade potential in this region, which will contribute to the sustainable growth of China – Latin American and the Caribbean economic and trade relations, as well as promote the upgrading of bilateral cooperation.

(3) Demand of Upgrading Infrastructure

Infrastructure is the prerequisite of resources and products export, and the poor infrastructure in Latin America has been the bottleneck of economic development. At present, there is an urgent need for infrastructure construction and industrialization in Latin America, and China, with sufficient amount of quality and cheap equipment and production capacity, has strong comprehensive capacity. As social development and environmental issues attract more attention, Latin American countries look forward to China's contribution to improve local living standards and employment rate through investing infrastructure and transportation. The participation in the infrastructure construction and industries in host countries is conducive to the long term development and in the interest of Chinese enterprises, which will in turn optimize the current single resource manufacturing structure in Latin America, and help China develop its equipment manufacturing industries and participate in international competition. ①

3.2 Production Capacity Cooperation Patterns between China and Latin America

Compared with trade cooperation, production capacity cooperation features deeper penetration, more demands, and wider range. Especially in some high – end equipment manufacturing industries, it is hard to develop in a short term without required equipment and technical talent staff. Therefore, in the process of industrial transfer between the two sides, China's advantages and surplus production capacity, the practical needs and production condition of Latin American and the Caribbean countries should be taken into account to seek the entry point of cooperation, and then promote overall cooperation, so as to help Latin American and the Caribbean countries optimize industrial chains and supporting by China's export of production capacity to Latin America. The pattern of production capacity cooperation between China and Latin America should be in accordance with the local characteristics. The above – mentioned measures are concrete steps to carry out overall cooperation, which means that production capacity cooperation between the two sides has a clear direction and specific path. In this way, the "upgraded version" of economic and trade cooperation between China and Latin America will be formed, which will boost world economic recovery. ② To be specific, production capacity cooperation can be realized through multiple channels, such as investment, trade, contracting projects, third – party cooperation, financing and establishment of industrial parks.

3.2.1 Investment

Production capacity cooperation is not the simple transfer of products between countries, but rather industrial output and production capacity transfer based on products transfer. Production capacity cooperation

① 李辉、吴笛：《我国对拉美直接投资发展的新趋势及对策建议》，《海外投资与出口信贷》2015年2月1日。

② 王子约：《"3乘3" 模式亮相 李克强再推国际产能合作》，《第一财经日报》2015年5月21日。

between China and Latin America should, starting from entry points, stimulate demands in supporting fields and downstream industries, so as to attract investment in upstream and downstream industries. Therefore, investment in the whole industrial chain in Latin America would be promoted, which will solve the problem of financing, develop technology and production capacity, as well as accelerate the industrial development. To achieve this goal, flexible ways of investment can be introduced, including large enterprises leading the medium and small ones, private enterprises cooperating with state – owned enterprises and the "huddling" of private enterprises. Consequently, a market community that enhances the ability of Chinese enterprises to withstand risks will be formed.

3.2.2 Trade

Successful trade relation between China and Latin America has been demonstrated by the expansion of bilateral trade volume over the past years. Imports from China include electrometrical equipment, chemical products, transportation equipment, communications equipment, steel and finished steel, plastics, rubber products, furniture and textiles. Owing to the good trade ties, many Chinese products have been accepted by the local market in Latin America, whose needs, in turn, have been understood by China. On this basis, qualified Chinese enterprises can be encouraged to set up factories in Latin America, so as to replace a part of export with local production. Therefore Chinese enterprises, whiling fulfilling the needs of local market and alleviating the employment tension in Latin America, can further tap the potential of local market, and promote the transfer of upstream and downstream industries to this region.

3.2.3 Financial Services

As financing support plays a crucial role in the "going out" of Chinese enterprises, outbound investment and production capacity cooperation, to conduct production capacity cooperation effectively, China needs to expand financing channels such as fund, credit and insurance, providing quality financial service for Chinese enterprises, combining financial capital with industrial capital to build a solid and reliable bridge for production capacity cooperation.

In recent years, some Latin American and the Caribbean countries have experienced by difficulties in financing, especially the lack of financing and financing channels. In view of this, Chinese financial institutions should step up its pace of "going out", and establish branches in this region to facilitate the financial service for Chinese enterprises. In terms of service modes, they need to be flexible and provide targeted services. For example, they may set up various funds to support bilateral cooperation on production capacity equipment, and finance cooperation projects by offering loans. Besides, Chinese financial institutions can give full play to their functions of link and support, and together with related enterprises, explore new business modes for joint outbound investment between financial capital and industrial capital. In September 2015, China – Latin America Production Capacity Cooperation Investment Fund was established. This fund, abiding by international economic and financial rules, will invest in various fields such as manufacturing, high – tech, agriculture, energy, mineral, infrastructure and financial cooperation by selling equities, issuing bonds and other methods, so as to realize the mid and long term financial sustainability.

In addition, financial institutions should improve their export credit insurance function, provide insurance for Chinese enterprises and equipment that "go out", and escort for Chinese enterprises that conduct international production capacity cooperation. In short, various Chinese financial institutions should serve as a bridge and pave the way for cooperation capacity cooperation between China and Latin America, increase financial support, and continuously improve the service quality in Latin America and even in the world.

3.2.4 Engineering Contract

Fruitful cooperation has been conducted in engineering contracts. Chinese enterprises have contracted a number of key projects, including the second phase of the ultra – high voltage electricity transmission project in the Belo Monte hydroelectric dam in Brazil, the construction of Argentina Bulgano freight railway, the construction of economical housing for the Mozambican government, power transmission project of Duo Kema in Venezuela. These projects have been acknowledged by Latin American and the Caribbean countries, and the Westmoreland bridge project and airport road project contracted by China Harbor Engineering Co, have won the first award of the Jamaican Project Prize. Projects contracts can be a good ice – breaking strategy for production capacity cooperation with Latin America. As the lack of finance remains the largest obstacle for a number of countries in this region, Chinese enterprises can provide reasonable financing plans and transform the contracted projects to invested ones. Moreover, the completion of key infrastructure projects will improve the local business index, generating numerous investment opportunities, which can be seized by contractors in advance.

3.2.5 Third – Party Cooperation

Chinese enterprises can conduct joint venture cooperation with international companies from developed countries to enter Latin American market and wait for the opportunity to expand independent investment in the region. Through this channel, the operation risks for Chinese enterprises will be reduced, and the needs of the local market will be understood, besides, China's development level will be improved and industrial upgrading will be realized because of the introduction of advanced technology and management skills from developed countries.

3.2.6 Establishing Industrial Parks

Latin American and the Caribbean countries look forward to not only the industrial transfer from China, but also China's development, construction and operation patterns of industrial parks. However, there haven't been coordinated industrial parks invested by China at this stage. Chinese enterprises can invest in and set up industrial parks, where the complete infrastructure will reduce the external cost. Chinese – funded industrial parks in Latin America will not only coordinate supply and demand, but also become a highlight in local production capacity cooperation. Besides, Chinese enterprises should also make efforts to jointly set up industrial parks with developed countries. Industrial parks should first be established for key industries and the key links of the industries in accordance with the local conditions, demands, and industrial development. Then the industrial parks can be introduced to the whole industrial chain when condition permits.

3.3 Fields Production Capacity Cooperation between China and Latin America

To realize the production capacity cooperation between China and Latin America, efforts should be made orderly in key industries such as building material, logistics, electricity, chemical, textile, automobile, communications, engineering machinery, aerospace, shipbuilding and maritime engineering.

3.3.1 Building Materials

As shown in Figure 3, China's investment potential indices in major Latin American and the Caribbean countries outnumber trade potential indices. Especially in Brazil, Mexico and Peru, the investment potential indices are much higher than these of trade. This demonstrates the large space for production capacity cooperation in building materials. In March, 2015, the 21st International Building Materials Exhibition was held in Brazil. 883 enterprises from 14 countries and regions participated in this exhibition, among which 345 enterprises were from mainland China, Hong Kong and Taiwan, accounting for 39% of the number of exhibitors. China is the main supplier of Brazil's hardware building materials market which features large scale, rapid growth, increasing external dependence and large potential for production capacity cooperation. Construction industry has long been the pillar of Brazilian economy. At present, with unprecedented challenges to Brazilian economy, Brazilian government pins hope on construction industry, and will soon implement new investment plans for logistics to stimulate growth in construction industry. Besides, Brazil will also promote the development of new energy and green materials in this industry.

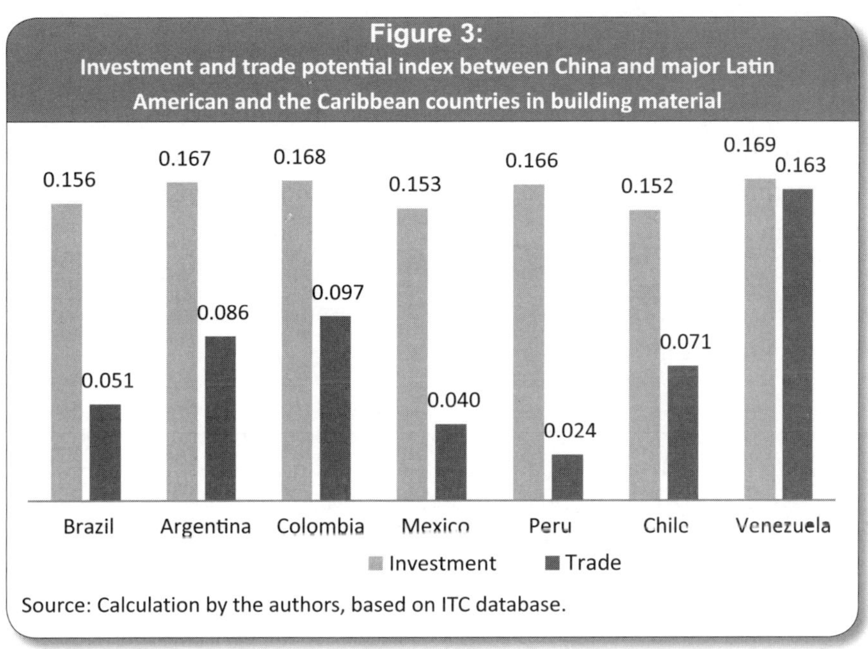

In accordance with its needs of internal industrial restructuring, China can give full play to its backbone enterprises in the industry and construction enterprises. While focusing on investment, China can introduce other methods such as design, construction and equipment supply in Latin American and the Caribbean countries with high demand and low production capacity. By setting up assembly lines in areas such as cement, flat glass, building sanitary ceramics, new building materials and new building, China can improve the industrial production capacity and increase market supply in Latin America.

3.3.2 Logistics and Infrastructure Construction

As shown in Figure 4, the investment potential indices between China and major Latin American and the Caribbean countries in infrastructure construction industry are positive, higher than trade potential indices. The large gap between the two indices in Brazil, Mexico and Peru indicates that there is a huge space for bilateral production capacity cooperation. Despite of rich resources and agricultural products, Latin America can hardly attract enough investment and shift its resource advantages into tradable commodities due to the lack of transportation such as railways and highways. The attraction of investment requires labor, equipment and effective transportation, and the lack of transportation will significantly increase the pre – investment costs of investors as it is difficult for the enterprises alone to build roads. Most of the mineral resources are located in mountain regions, distant from ports and main traffic routes; besides, confidence of investors is insufficient due to the slump in global commodity prices. In light of this, local governments should improve the investment environment to support investors.

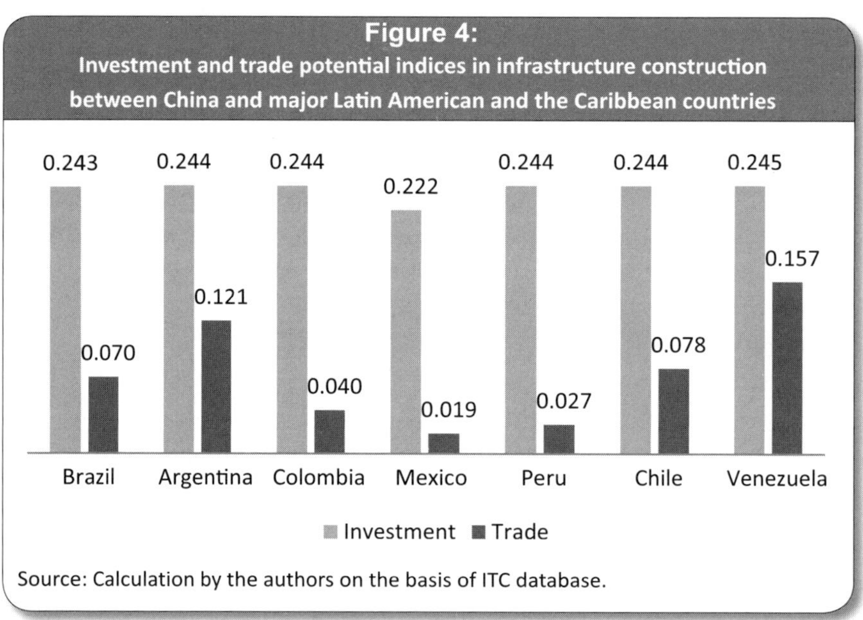

According to the *Guideline on Promoting International Production Capacity Cooperation and Equipment Manufacturing Cooperation* issued by the State Council, the "going out" of railways should be accelerated. To conduct package cooperation on railways, China needs to give play to its advantages in design, construction, equipment supply, operation, maintenance, and financing. Cooperation on Twin Ocean Railroad Connection Project (hereinafter referred to as Twin Railroad) between China and Brazil will serve as the springboard of China's railway technology and equipment to the world market. In 2015, the joint statement issued by China and Brazil stressed the "vital importance" of railway cooperation to the integrated and sustainable infrastructure network in South America, and congratulated on China – Brazil – Peru working group embarking on the basic research of feasibility of the Twin Railroad. This is the substantial progress of the project. Connecting the Atlantic and the Pacific, the Twin Railroad runs across Brazil and Peru, and spans the Andes, the world's longest mountain chain. When completed, the Twin Railroad will benefit both China and Brazil: China can import products such as iron ore and soybeans from the Brazil through this new channel instead of going through the Panama Canal, which will improve transport efficiency; Brazil can promote its connectivity with Asia – Pacific region and stimulate export by reducing transport cost. In fact, progress has already been made in China – Brazil railway cooperation. Rio de Janeiro, a major Brazilian city, has imported 604 subway trains and metro trains from China. Besides, Brazil has ordered 90 subway trains from China for Olympic Games.

Construction of transport infrastructure should give priority to the promotion of connectivity with surrounding railways, construction of network in key regions and high – speed railways. China and countries in Latin America should actively develop and implement urban rail transit projects, expand international cooperation on urban rail transit vehicles, and establish service centers and R&D centers, so as to accelerate the integration of rail transport equipment enterprises and enhance the international operating strength as well as the comprehensive strength of backbone enterprises.

3.3.3 Electricity Projects

As shown in Figure 5, the investment potential indices between China and major Latin American and the Caribbean countries in electrical equipment are positive, higher than trade potential indices, indicating huge potential of production capacity cooperation. With 33 countries, Latin America is one of the largest regional electricity market, and also the international market that Chinese enterprises actively explore. Abundant in water resources, sunshine and bio – energy, Latin America has a huge energy gap. Statistics show that for new energy alone, from 2013 to 2030, Latin America needs at least 350 billion dollars to meet future needs. Under the joint framework in Latin America, foreign ministries of Chile, Bolivia, Colombia, Ecuador and Peru as well as Inter – American Development Bank are now conducting researches on the technical plan for network among the five countries and promoting the construction of network that covers the entire region. It is predicted that the sales volume of smart meters alone will reach 24 billion dollars, and two thirds of which may be achieved in Brazilian market.

Figure 5:
Investment and trade potential index in electrical equipment between China and Latin American and the Caribbean countries

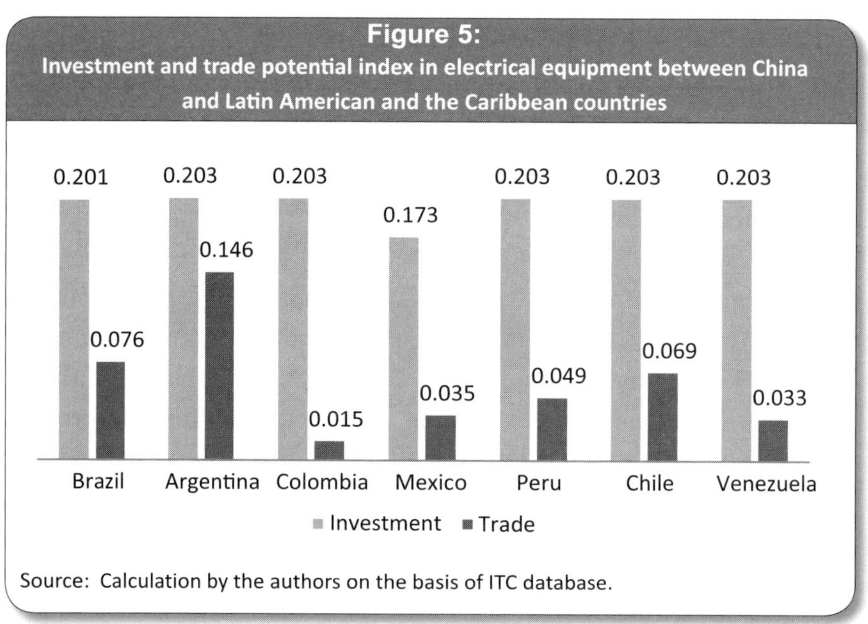

Source: Calculation by the authors on the basis of ITC database.

In recent years, Chinese government has introduced a number of favorable policies to explore Latin American and the Caribbean market. Chinese enterprises such as Power Construction Corporation of China, China International Water & Electric Corporation, State Grid Corporation of China, China Three Gorges Corporation and Yingli Group have gradually opened the electricity market in Latin America. China needs to encourage the "going out" of Chinese electricity enterprises, actively explore the thermal power and hydropower market, and expand Chinese thermal power and hydropower equipment and technology export by participating in cooperation on major electricity projects. In terms of nuclear power, China can carry out exchange and dialogues with Latin American and the Caribbean countries, promote cooperation on key projects and export of nuclear complete equipment and technology. In the fields of wind power and solar power, China can participate in the investment and construction in related projects, promoting cooperation on wind power and photovoltaic power production capacity and equipment. Besides, China also needs to invest in the construction and operation of overseas power grid projects, promoting the export of power transmission equipment.

3.3.4 Petrochemical Industry

As shown in Figure 6, the investment potential indices between China and major Latin American and the Caribbean countries in chemical industry are positive. Owing to the facilitation of resource supply, Mexico, Brazil and Argentina are doing well in petrochemical industry and have been acknowledged by the world. Currently, the problem of Mexico is the insufficient supply of resources, which can be solved by the development of Mexico's energy reform. The investment in petroleum and natural gas projects by private capital will reduce the price of resources that are crucial for the development. When Mexico completes its energy reform, the output of petroleum and gas will be increased greatly, which will stimulate the expansion of investment by providing sufficient supply for petrochemical industry. In comparison, the future of Argentina's petrochemical industry depends to a large extent on the government. Argentina needs to develop transparent policies to attract investment and ensure the stable resource supply for petrochemical industry. In the first decade of the 21st century, the sustained decline in oil and gas output has resulted in the short supply of petrochemical products. But with the development of Vaca Muerta, a giant shale oil and gas field, the petrochemical industry may possibly be revitalized. With 661 billion barrels of oil and 1181 trillion cubic feet of natural gas resources in stock, Vaca Muerta is considered as one of the world's most promising shale oil and gas zone.

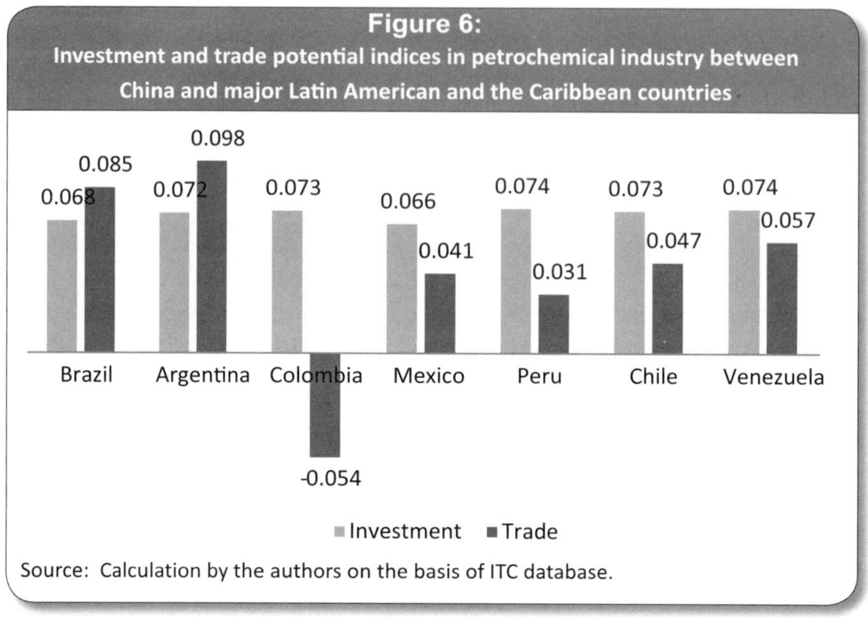

As global oil prices plunged in 2015, China reduced its investment in countries that depended on oil export such as Venezuela and Ecuador, and increased investment in other countries such as Brazil and Chile. In Latin American and the Caribbean countries with high demand and rich resources, China is leveraging its advantages in technology and production capacity, and expanding resource development and industrial investment by developing production lines of petrochemical, fertilizer, pesticides, tires and coal chemical. China will also give priority to meeting the needs of local market, and extend the industrial line by carrying out intensive process in downstream industries and establishing green production base, so as to increase export of complete equipment.

3.3.5 Textile Industry

Figure 7 shows that the investment potential indices in textile industry between China and major countries in Latin America are all positive, higher than trade potential indices. Latin America has geographical advantages: adjoining terminal markets such as the United States and Europe, Latin America has obvious transport advantages; developed maritime routes connect this region with the world's three major markets such as Asia – Pacific, the United States and Europe. Latin America has developed complete free trade network with them by free trade agreement and preferential agreements for investment, thus providing an easy access to European and the U.S. market. Therefore, Chinese enterprises that are charged with dumping in the U.S. can set up factories in Mexico as it adjoins the U.S., and enter the U.S. market directly with greatly reduced transport costs. The U.S. has signed free trade agreements with Mexico, Central American Community, Colombia, Peru and Chile. Having signed free trade agreements with Mexico, Chile and Central American Community, the EU is working on initiating the package free trade negotiation with MERCOSuR that covers Brazil, Argentina, Uruguay and Paraguay. Japan and South Korea are embarking on free trade negotiations or signing agreements with Latin American and the Caribbean countries such as Mexico and Chile, as the preferential trade arrangements and convenient transport have made Latin America one of the main destinations for investment from the EU, Japan and the South Korea.

Figure 7:
Investment and trade potential indices in textile industry between China and major Latin American and the Caribbean countries

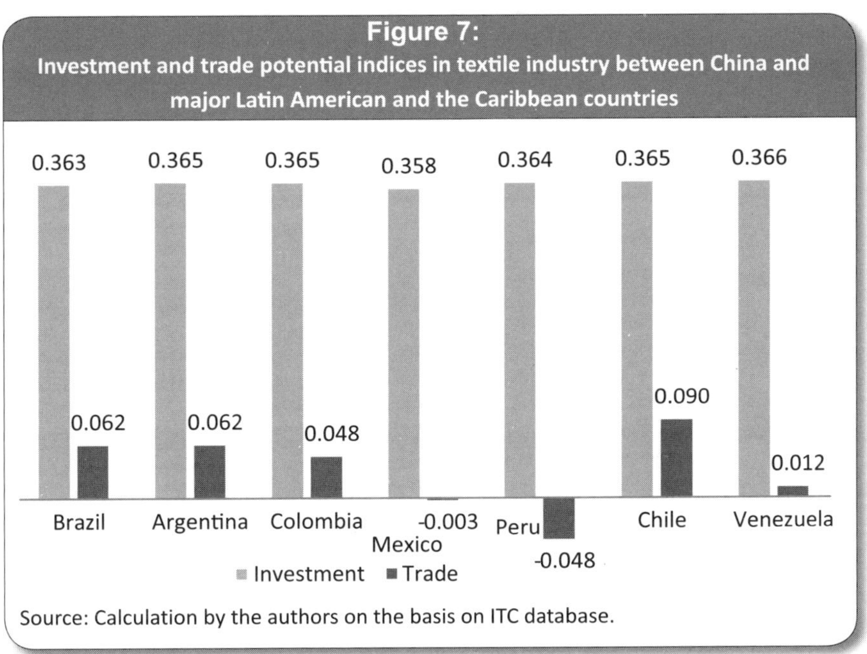

Source: Calculation by the authors on the basis on ITC database.

Having strong competitive advantages in textile industry, China can invest in cotton and chemical fiber industries in Latin American and the Caribbean countries that are abundant in labor resources, low production costs and convenient routes to the target markets. China can establish textile production base in industrial parks that have good conditions, and achieve cluster development by matching the upstream and downstream industries. China should also be rational about the progress and the scale of cooperation to synergize international cooperation with domestic industrial upgrading.

3.3.6 Automobile Industry

As shown in Figure 8, the investment potential indices in transport equipment industry between China and Latin American and the Caribbean countries are all positive, higher than trade potential indices, demonstrating huge potential for cooperation between China and Latin America in this field. At present, Chinese domestic automobile brands have entered the Argentinean market and the Brazilian market. For example, Chery, a Chinese auto brand, has invested and produced cars in Argentina, and some of its models were even listed as local best sellers. Automobile industry has always been one of the pillars of Mexican economy. Since joining the North American Free Trade Area and opened its market in 1994, Mexico has now become the fifth largest automobile producer, ranking only after Japan, the United States, the EU and Canada. Mexican government has made preferential policies for the development of automobile industry, and its cheap labor ensures the profit of manufacturers. Therefore, more and more automobile manufacturers are building factories in Mexico, which in turn contributes to the phenomenal growth of automobile industry in Mexico.

As automobile industry is estimated to achieve explosive development in Latin America, China should seize the opportunity and explore the automobile market, promoting the export of buses, trucks, minibuses and light buses. Chinese enterprises can set up production and assembly factories in Latin American and the Caribbean countries with huge market potential and complete associated industries, and establish distribution network and

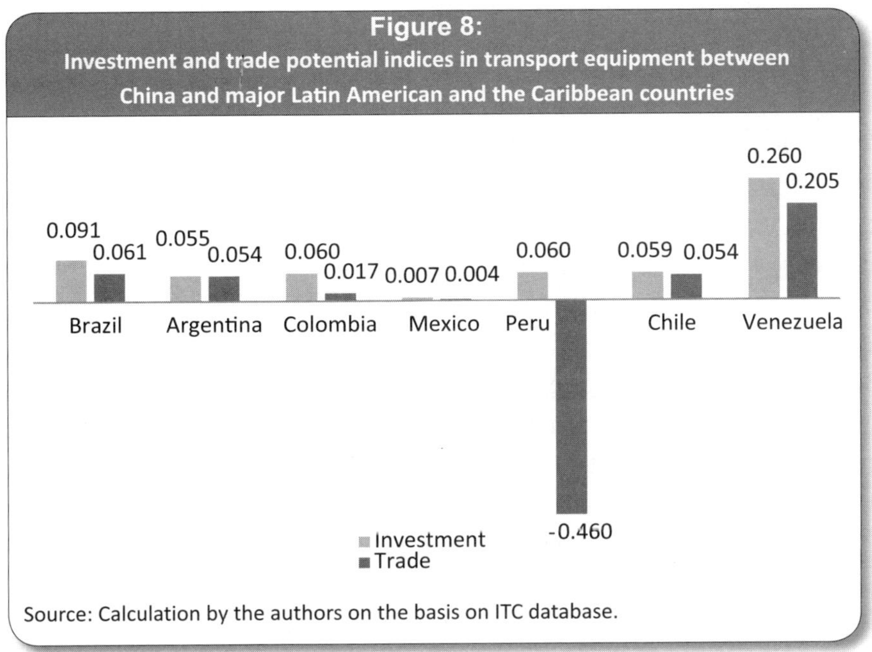

service centers to promote the export of vehicles and automobile parts, and to enhance the brand influence. China needs to encourage its enterprises to join hands with their counterparts from developed countries and set up technology and R&D centers in Latin America, so as to improve its capacity to develop and produce automobiles through cooperation with overseas enterprises that have strong technical strength.

3.3.7 Information and Communications Industry

As shown in Figure 9, the investment potential indices in information and communications industry between China and major countries in Latin America are positive and higher than trade potential indices. This indicates huge potential of cooperation between China and Latin America on information and communications industry. As the major supplier of products and services for Latin America, Chinese telecommunications enterprises begin to cooperate with European operators and participate in the development of new – generation of network and technical standards. In Latin American and the Caribbean market, sales of Samsung mobile phones, a South Korean brand, has dropped sharply, while the sales of China's products shows robust growth. Huawei is one of the Chinese enterprises that first "went out", and its development in Latin America has been widely acknowledged by the local market. At present, Huawei has established 14 branches or representative offices in this region, with services ranging from home network to corporate communications and terminal products. Besides, Huawei has participated in six seventh of the 4G network construction in Brazil. It is fair to say that Huawei is ubiquitous in Latin America. ZET, another Chinese communications enterprise, has developed through cooperation with local governments, providing technical support for construction in fields such as transportation, education and electricity.

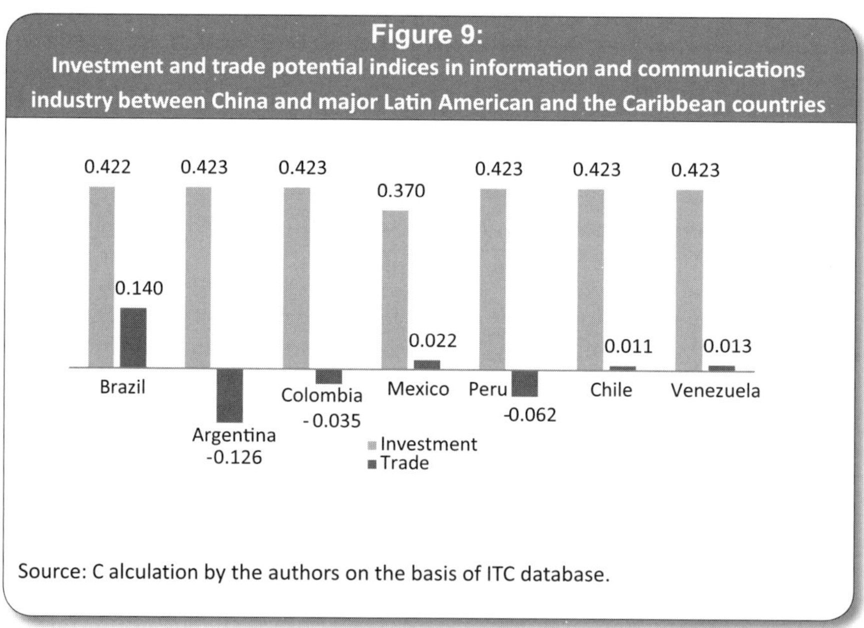

Figure 9: Investment and trade potential indices in information and communications industry between China and major Latin American and the Caribbean countries

Source: C alculation by the authors on the basis of ITC database.

As an emerging market, Latin America has varied demands, boosting huge development potential. Advanced in information and communications technology and services, Chinese enterprises are capable of fulfilling these demands. China needs to give full play to its competitive edge of large – scale communications and network equipment manufacturing enterprises, and expand Latin American and the Caribbean market. Chinese enterprises should be market – oriented, center on users, and strengthen cooperation with local operators and group users so as to improve global competitiveness through enhancing design, development, technical support, operation maintenance and information security. China needs to encourage the “going out” of telecommunications operation enterprises and Internet companies through multiple channels such as merger, acquisition, investment and facility operation. Now European telecommunications companies account for a large share of local market, and Chinese enterprises can enter the market through cooperating with European counterparts. The combination of China’s technology and products and Europe’s talents will give them the leading position in the local market. Specifically, Chinese enterprises can conduct cooperation through establishing infrastructures such as information operation networks and data centers. China needs to encourage its enterprises to set up R&D centers overseas, and enhance research and development of new information technology by using global intellectual resources.

3.3.8 Engineering Machinery Industry

As shown in Figure 10, the investment potential indices in engineering machinery industry between China and major Latin American and the Caribbean countries are positive, demonstrating huge potential for engineering machinery cooperation between China and Latin America. According to a report issued by a Chilean investment consultative agency, Chile, Peru, Colombia and Brazil will invest 500.8 billion dollars in infrastructure from 2012 to 2021, giving priority to transportation, municipal facilities, telecommunications, drinking water, health facilities, water conservancy facilities and intercity high – ways. Most of the projects are jointly invested and open to foreign investment. The huge demand for engineering equipment such as pavement, earthwork and concrete will provide Chinese enterprises a golden opportunity.

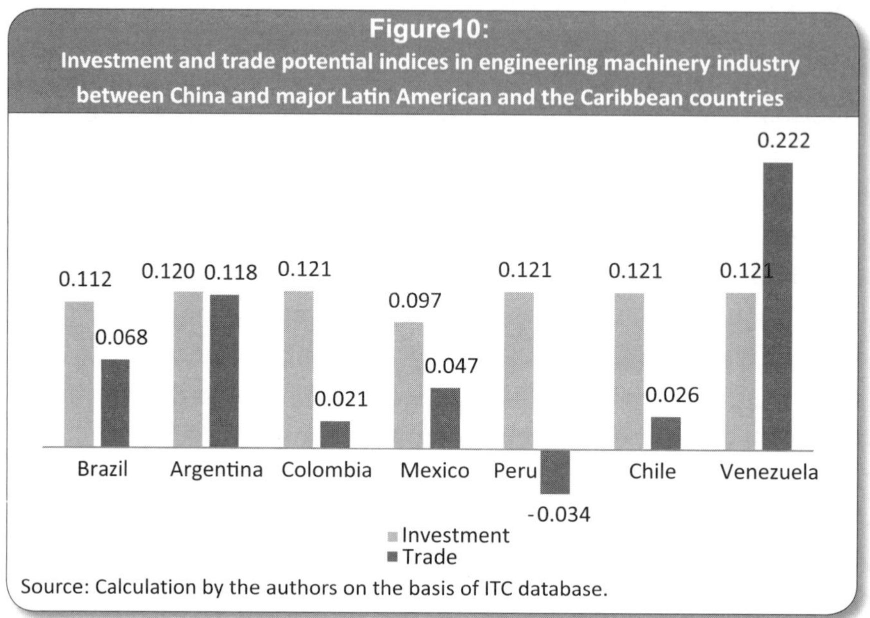

Chinese enterprises in fields such as engineering machinery, agricultural machinery, oil equipment and machine tools need to make more efforts to explore the market. Specifically, they can provide financial leasing services and expand export by carrying out major overseas construction projects. China needs to encourage enterprises to set up factories in countries that have favorable conditions, and complete the construction of operation and maintenance networks, so as to improve comprehensive competitiveness. For example, in 2011, Xuzhou Construction Machinery Group invested 200 million dollars in MG, Brazil to build XCMG engineering machinery industrial park with an area of 80,000 square meters, in order to build its first overseas manufacturing base for complete sets of engineering equipment. Earlier than that, Sany Heavy Industry opened a branch office in Brazil in 2007, and invested 200 million dollars to set up factories locally in 2010. Now Sany is planning to set up 6S shops of engineering machinery in Brazil. Chinese government needs to its enterprises to cooperate with foreign companies with advantages in brand, technology and market, and establish R&D centers in developed countries to improve brand influence and technical strength.

3.3.9 Aerospace Industry

As shown in Figure 11, the investment potential indices in aerospace industry between China and major countries in Latin America are positive, higher than trade potential indices. This demonstrates huge potential for cooperation between China and Latin America on transport equipment. With its rapid growth in aerospace, helicopter market of Latin America has become an important destination for world aircraft manufacturers. Statistics show that in five years, the current helicopter unit will be expanded by 34%. Therefore, China needs to vigorously expand aviation market in developing countries, set up joint – ventured aviation enterprises in Latin American and the Caribbean, establish logistics base, and gradually make the regional network of aviation transport. Chinese enterprises can accelerate aviation cooperation with Latin American and the Caribbean countries and set up regional aviation centers that radiate neighboring countries, so as to promote the export of domestic aircrafts. By supporting the dominant aviation enterprises to invest in advanced manufacturers and R&D centers, China can promote the quality of domestic aircrafts. China can actively promote its external launch services by enhancing aerospace cooperation with Latin American and the Caribbean countries. In terms of satellite, China needs to cooperate with developed countries in fields such as satellite design, parts manufacturing and payload development, and encourage qualified enterprises to invest in foreign enterprises with unique characteristics.

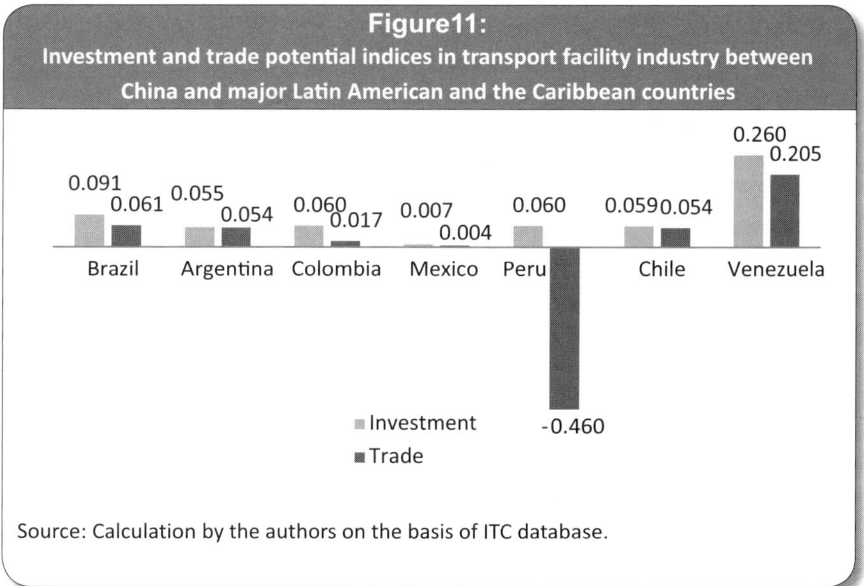

3.3.10. Ships and Marine Engineering Equipment Industry

As shown in Figure 12, the investment potential indices in transport equipment are positive, higher than trade potential indices, indicating huge potential for cooperation between China and Latin America on transport equipment. In recent years, China has achieved great progress in marine engineering equipment. In particular, China has laid a solid foundation in oil and gas development equipment, with annual sales volume exceeding 30 billion, accounting for nearly 7% of the world market share. China has basically achieved independent design of shallow oil and gas equipment, and some of its marine engineering ships have become branded, besides, breakthroughs have been made in deep – sea equipment manufacturing.

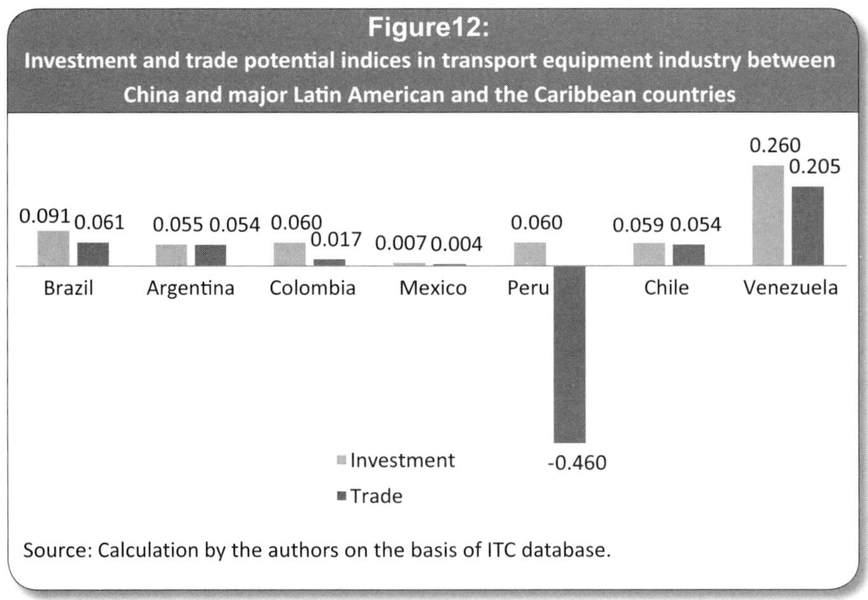

There is a huge demand for ships and marine engineering equipment in Latin America. For example, Brazil, rich in deep water oil and gas resources, is one of the major markets for deep water semi – submersible platforms, accounting for one fourth of the world market share. With the discovery of Brazil's largest deep water salt oil field at the end of 2017, larger demand for marine engineering equipment has been generated, making Brazil the potentially largest destination of investment in marine engineering equipment. In 2006, as a global supplier of logistics equipment and services, China International Marine Containers (Group) Co. LTD, under the guidance of "going out" strategy, entered the Brazilian market through partnerships with local enterprises, and became one of the overseas suppliers of equipment for oil states such as Brazil. Now Latin America has become one of its core business areas.

Other oil states such Mexico and Venezuela also boast huge market demand. For example, along the north shore of the Gulf of Mexico, marine equipment industry has been monopolized by large international oil companies, leaving little room for other enterprises. But on the other side of the Gulf, the market is to be explored, which needs a great number of equipment and technology, providing golden opportunities for enterprises. Due to its sluggish economy, Mexico welcomes international companies to promote the development of domestic oil. At present, two of Mexican semi – submersible platforms are also in bidding.

Despite of its development in independent design and key technologies in marine equipment, China lags behind enterprises from developed countries that entered Latin American and the Caribbean market earlier. The gap is mainly reflected in R&D capability and innovation strength. Weak in supporting capacity, Chinese enterprises rely heavily on import of core technologies, and hasn't fostered the professional manufacturing ability with international competitiveness, resulting in the fact that they are still at the low – end of industrial chain. To reverse the situation, China needs to leverage its advantages in ship production capacity, and vigorously explore high – end ship and marine engineering equipment market while consolidating its status in the mid and low – end market. By supporting qualified enterprises invest in and set up factories, overseas R&D centers and sales & service offices, China can improve its ability of developing and manufacturing high – end ships, and promote the international competitiveness of products such as deep water semi – submersible drilling platforms, floating production and storage devices, marine engineering ships, liquefied natural gas vessels.

3.4 Coordination of RMB Internationalization and Production Capacity Cooperation between China and Latin America

RMB internationalization is conducive to the better integration of

Chinese economy into the world economy, strengthening the market mechanism, improving the effective allocation of resources, promoting international monetary system reform and maintaining the stability of global financial market. In addition, RMB internationalization will increase China's influence on and voice in global economic activities. Production capacity cooperation between China and Latin America can promote the upgrading of China's economy, and prolong its industrial chain by the use of natural resources of Latin America. RMB internationalization and the production capacity cooperation support each other and will achieve coordinated development in the future.

3.4.1 Development of RMB Internationalization

As China's economy entered the new normal, the growth pattern of it has undergone marked shift. The implementation and expansion of "Belt and Road Initiative" as well as the deepening of "going out" strategy have contributed to the transformation of China's foreign trade structure from trade – oriented to investment – oriented, and to the export of capital, which inevitably requires RMB internationalization. As a symbol of China's rise and one of the indicators of Chinese comprehensive competitiveness, RMB internationalization is a core part of "Chinese Dream", and is closely related to China's overall economic and financial development.

The process RMB internationalization did not start until after the global financial recession. However, the level of international use of RMB has registered continuously rapid growth since the establishment of RMB cross – border trade settlement pilots in 2009. With the improvement of cross – border RMB policies and clearing arrangements, as well as the expansion of offshore market, RMB has been increasingly accepted in international trade, financial transactions and as foreign exchange reserve, which raised the level of RMB internationalization remarkably. According to statistics of *Report on RMB Internationalization 2015* issued by Renmin University of China, RMB Internationalization Index (hereinafter referred to as RII) has risen from 0.02% in 2009 to 2.47% in 2014, an increase of 45.4% (see Figure 13). As RII gradually improved, RMB has narrowed the gap with yen and pound, and is likely to surpass yen and become the world's fourth largest international currency.

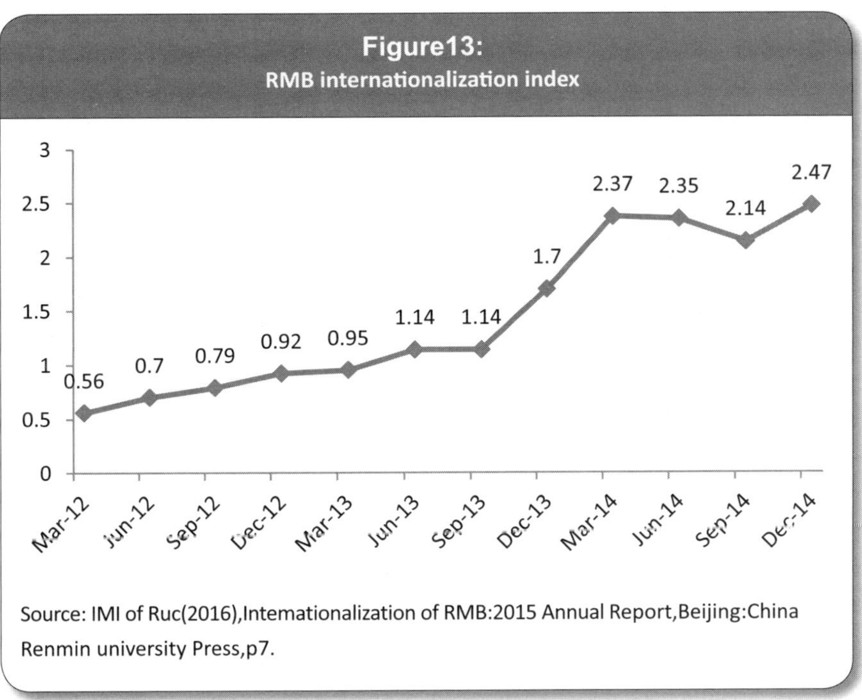

Figure13:
RMB internationalization index

Source: IMI of Ruc(2016),Intemationalization of RMB:2015 Annual Report,Beijing:China Renmin university Press,p7.

Consequently, market expectations of RMB internationalization also improved greatly. According to Bank of China's survey on overseas enterprises, 41% of overseas enterprises in China hold that "RMB is likely to be an important international currency, and its status and function may be close to that of US dollar and the euro" in 2014, an increase of 10% on the previous year; the proportion of enterprises that thought "the international status and role of RMB is hard to assessed" dropped by 4%, indicating that more and more overseas enterprises in China hold a positive idea towards the prospect and role of RMB as an international currency (see Figure 14). In comparison, domestic enterprises have more positive expectations of RMB's role in China's foreign trade settlement: the proportion of domestic enterprises holding that RMB will be used in more than 40% of foreign trade is 40%, 7% higher than that of 2013; the proportion of domestic enterprises thinking that RMB will be used in 20% to 30% is 33%, an increase of 7% over 2913.

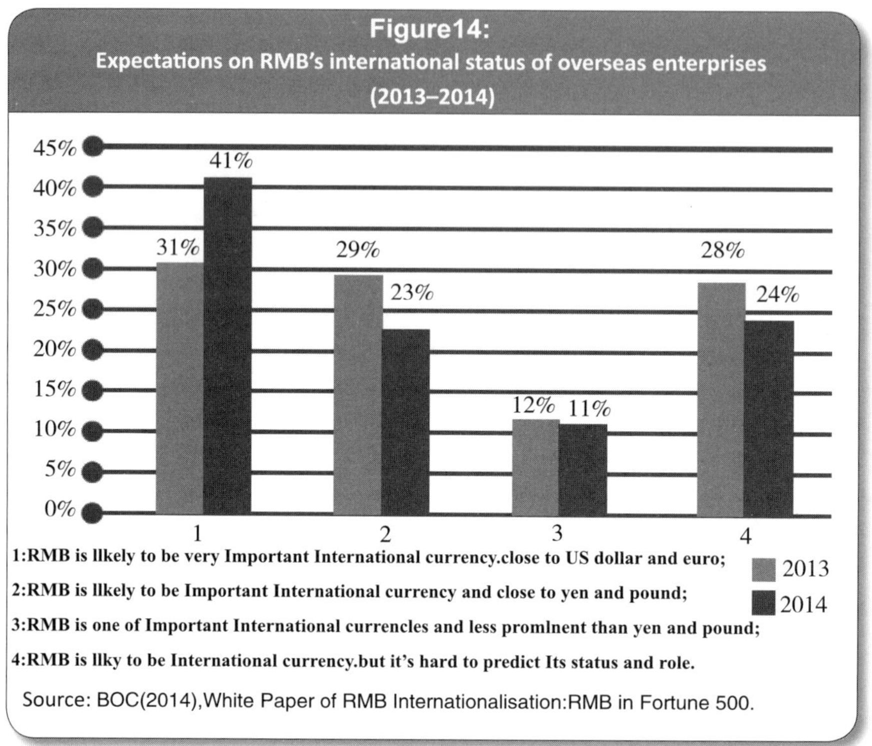

Figure14:
Expectations on RMB's international status of overseas enterprises (2013–2014)

Source: BOC(2014),White Paper of RMB Internationalisation:RMB in Fortune 500.

On December 1, 2015, the IMF announced RMB's inclusion in the basket of SDR, marking that RMB was recognized by the IMF as an international reserve currency. According to statistics from Society for Worldwide Interbank Financial Telecommunications (SWIFT), RMB maintained its status as the second largest international funding currency, the 5th largest payment currency, the 6th foreign exchange trade currency and international interbank loan currency in the second quarter of 2015. ① According to *Review of the Method of the Valuation of the SDR – Initial Considerations*, a report issued by the IMF in 2015, regardless of low level of its international use, RMB internationalization has achieved significant progress compared with other currencies during the same period.

The minimum objective of RMB internationalization is to help

① Xing Yujing & Zeng Yuanyuan, "The Recent Progress of RMB Internationalisation" , *China Finance*, lssue 16, 2015, p.13.

China avoid the damages of volatility in international exchange rates and the uncertainty of dollar system. According to structuralism theory, "peripheral countries" in the world economy, due to the lack of long – term credit base and a sound local capital market, cannot avoid the mismatch of currency and time as they can only accumulate debt or assets in US dollar rather than domestic currency. Therefore, the economy of these countries is affected by international business cycles and unfavorable speculation. However, developing countries can only adapt to the situation or expect the improvement of the international monetary system. As the leader of emerging economies, through RMB settlement, clearing and payment, China can cover the majority of losses caused by volatility in exchange rates and US dollar crisis, so as to gain international competitiveness. With this objective being achieved, China is likely to become a global financial power and perform its functions of "world bank" such as providing short – term liquidity for global economic activities, achieving the effective allocation of capital worldwide and promote the balanced development of world economy.

3.4.2 RMB Internationalization and Production Capacity Cooperation between China and Latin America: Coordinated Development

As an indispensable part of national development strategy, RMB internationalization and production capacity cooperation between China and Latin America are important measures that China take to provide global public goods and help Latin American and the Caribbean countries to realize the economic restructuring and transformation, which embodies China's sense of responsibility as a big country. Due to the institutional defects of international institutions and the decline of US economic strength, problems such as the serious shortage of global public goods and imbalanced structures arise. The weakening of US dollar dominance of contributed to the upsurge of risks in dollar assets, posing a threat to the stability and development of world economy and finance. As one of the emerging markets and developing countries, China is capable of shouldering its responsibility and playing a bigger role in global economic governance by providing global public goods. With the operation of China – Latin American and the Caribbean Cooperation

Fund and the Sino – Latin American and the Caribbean Production Capacity Cooperation, the cooperation models and concepts between the two sides have been updated, and China's capital has been highly synergized with resources of Latin American and the Caribbean. The adherence to the comparative advantages and the extending of the value chains can contribute to the building of community of shared future of China and Latin America. China, as the initiator and promoter of production capacity cooperation between China and Latin America, will step up to realize the phase objective of RMB internationalization by the functions of RMB as an international currency.

As the driving force for China's industrial upgrading and the coordinated development in a broader region and worldwide, production capacity cooperation between China and Latin America will not only improve the development of real economy for both sides, but also promote RMB internationalization and provide a new way for China's financial strategy. The implementation and promotion of production capacity cooperation will deepen financial cooperation, and enhance the role of RMB in trade settlement, currency exchanges and investment credit. This will contribute to RMB internationalization and global currency system reform, and explore new development path for economy and finance. RMB internationalization and production capacity cooperation are not only in line with China's national interests, but can also uphold the sustainable economic development and the transformation and upgrading of industrial structure and export structure in Latin America, thus further improving the current world economic order and international monetary system.

First of all, production capacity cooperation between China and Latin America will further facilitate the regional use and global promotion of RMB. Production capacity cooperation requires the complementarity between China and Latin American and the Caribbean countries in fields such as strategies, infrastructure, trade and financing, which demands enhanced economic cooperation, and a deepened regional cooperation pattern that effectively matches the market demands and supplies. Currently, there are certain defects in China – Latin American and the Caribbean trade structure, which is embodied by the fact that many Latin American and the Caribbean scholars frequently criticize China of importing only resource – intensive products from Latin America and occupying market share that originally belonged to local enterprises by exporting industrial manufactured products. In addition, Argentina, Chile, Brazil and Colombia are among the countries that file anti – dumping lawsuits most frequently against China every year (see Table 2). Production capacity cooperation will realize RMB internationalization by extending the industrial chains of Latin America and promoting industrial upgrading.

Table 2:
Anti – dumping against China in Latin America
(1995–2013)

	Anti – dumping (case)	**Anti – dumping Against China (case)**	**Proportion of lawsuit against China(%)**	**Global anti – dumping intensity (%)**	**Intensity of anti – dumping against China(%)**
Brazil	334	78	23.35	1027	2435
Argentina	312	90	28.85	2885	8266
Mexico	115	40	34.78	175	648
Colombia	67	36	53.73	862	4370
Peru	72	22	30.56	1394	3249

Source: Liang Junwei & Dai Zhongqiang(2015), “Dynamics of Developing Countries’ Antidumping:Macro & Micro Perspectives” , *Internatcoral Economics,* Issue 11,p9.

Besides, the increased level of RMB internationalization will in turn promote the scale and results of production capacity cooperation. The exchange rate risks in trade of goods can be avoided by the use of local currency rather than a third – party currency in settlement, which will directly benefit both importers and exporters. As the US dollar is still the major international settlement currency, Chinese exporters and Latin American and the Caribbean importers need to exchange twice, which means both sides will be exposed to great risks if they don’t conduct hedge transactions. China’s surplus production capacity can be transformed to the solid material basis for cooperation through multiple channels such as RMB bonds, loans and direct investment, which will provide financial support for production capacity cooperation between

China and Latin America. Furthermore, the use of RMB in direct pricing will create a new international mechanism for currency and risk management, so as to maintain economic and financial stability in Latin America.

3.4.3 Production Capacity Cooperation between China and Latin America Promotes RMB Internationalization

Researches indicate despite of rapid growth of its internationalization, RMB is not yet qualified to replace the local currency and US dollar due to some historical and realistic reasons. ① Progress in production capacity cooperation will make breakthroughs for RMB internationalization in this region through channels such as commodity pricing and settlement, infrastructure financing and construction of industrial parks. Taking Latin American and the Caribbean countries as destination for RMB internationalization, China needs to seize the opportunity, constantly enrich financial products and commodities that are denominated in RMB, increase investment opportunities for RMB, and boosted RMB as reserve currency of some countries by the innovation of RMB products.

First of all, the use of RMB in commodity pricing and settlement among Latin American and the Caribbean countries will become a break – through for RMB internationalization. The economic aggregate of Latin America was 6 trillion US dollars in 2013, with per capita GDP reaching 9,881 US dollars, and the per capital GDP of major countries such as Chile, Argentina and Brazil exceeded 10,000 dollars, indicating considerable market capacity. In 2014, bilateral trade volume between China and Latin America was 263.6 billion dollars, contributed mainly by commodity trade in fields such as food, energy, agricultural raw materials and metal. According to United Nations Economic Commission for Latin America, every 1 percentage point growth of Chinese economy would pull Latin American and the Caribbean economy by 0.5 percentage point. In this light, cooperation in trade, investment and finance between China and Latin America will be an important driving force for further improvement of China's international competitiveness and involvement

① Chai Yu , "RMB Internationalisation and A Survey of Latin America for Farget Aree" , *World Economics & Politics*, Issue 4, 2013, p101.

in the restructuring of global production chain. The use of RMB in commodity pricing and settlement of bilateral trade will contribute to the development of bilateral trade and economic growth. In recent years, Export – Import Bank of China continuously promoted cross – border RMB use and financing business, and vigorously encouraged its customers to use RMB in cross – border business. To date, RMB loans issued by the Export – Import Bank of China accounts for over 60% of its total loans, and RMB's proportion in its overseas projects has registered consistent growth. Consequently, the balance of cross – border RMB loans outnumbers that of other banks. Owing to the fast growth of the scale of RMB assets, the market influence of RMB upsurge: in 2010, RMB ranked the 28th in the trading volume of domestic currency, and the 21st in 2011; in 2012, it ranked the 11th, with trading volume exceeding 1 billion dollars. ①

Besides, RMB is expected to be one of the key currencies for production capacity cooperation between China and Latin America and infrastructure financing. According to World Bank's survey on enterprises, among enterprises from six regions in the world, more than 50% local enterprises of Latin America hold that the infrastructure in this region is poor, outnumbering the proportion in other enterprises. ② According to the rankings of IMF on the infrastructure quality indicators among five regions in the world, the average ranking of Latin America is the 80th among 134 countries, only higher than that of Sub – Saharan African. ③ In addition, the infrastructure construction of five major countries in Latin America is relatively backward in the list of global competitiveness issued by The World Economic Forum. ④ Among 144 sample countries, Brazil, Colombia, Peru and Argentina ranked the 76th, 84th, 88th and 89th respectively; Chile, the highest in the five countries, ranked only the 49th. The funding gap in Latin American and the Caribbean infrastructure construction will provide more opportunities for capitals from China, whose technologies and large – scale savings

① China EXIM Bank, "RMB Financing Operations", http://www.eximbank.gov.cn/tm/second/index_44.html.

② CAF – Latin America Development Bank, *Toward Furture:Management of Latin American Infractructare*, Beijing:Contemporary World Press, p20.

③ Ibid..

④ http://www.weforum.org/reports/global – competitiveness – report–2014–2015.

enable it to be the organizer and financial provider for infrastructure financing system in Latin America. In the future, China needs to enhance the engagement of RMB in infrastructure projects in Latin America and make it a common international currency. To achieve this goal, China needs to increase RMB products in foreign aid, outbound investment and project loans, and gradually improve the utilization rate of RMB in multilateral financial institutions such as BRICS Development Bank; besides, China can encourage the use of RMB in pricing and settlement through multiple channels such as domestic and foreign public – private partnership, syndicated loans and industrial investment fund; on the basis of China – Brazil and China – Argentina currency swap agreements, China can deepen the currency swap cooperation, and increase the capital for the construction of technical facilities by involving the swap of RMB in the local credit system.

At last, the construction of industrial parks in host countries can be an important driving force for RMB internationalization. As the third largest global investor, China is the biggest foreign investor for many Latin American and the Caribbean countries. If China builds industrial parks in various fields in Latin American and the Caribbean countries, the proportion of its investment in these countries will increase greatly, which will expand the overall investment. This will not only help Latin American and the Caribbean countries break the bottle neck of capital, but also promote production capacity cooperation between China and Latin America comprehensively, and effectively support the RMB internationalization. In order to meet the demands for financing and trading settlement in the early phase of construction and operations in the industrial parks, Chinese financial institutions will be stationed in the industrial parks to develop related RMB financial products and improve the proportion of RMB utilization locally. To realize this goal, non – commercial banks need to support financially, and make due contribution to the upfront investment and maintenance of industrial parks. With the development of industrial parks, financial institutions will expand its business step and step from the basic financial services to a multi – level and all – round support system, so as to form a global RMB exchange network by establishing RMB offshore market.

Report Three

The Cooperation of Infrastructure Construction between China and Latin America from the Perspective of the Belt and Road Initiative: Taking the Cooperation of Railway Construction between China and South America as an Example

Xie Wenze

The China – Latin America and the Caribbean Partnership (Latin America) has entered into a new stage of overall cooperation. The framework of the overall cooperation has basically been clear, with the guiding thought of "Five in One", one plan [China – Latin American and Caribbean Countries Cooperation Plan (2015–2019)], 2 aims (the aim of increasing bilateral trade volume between China and Latin America reach to $500 billion in 10 years from 2015, and the aim of raising the stock of reciprocal investment to at least 250 billion US dollars in 10 years from 2015), 3 mechanisms (trade, investment and financial cooperation), 6 cooperation priorities (energy and resources, infrastructure construction, agriculture, manufacturing, scientific and technological innovation and information technology), "3×3" model for capacity cooperation (which refers to jointly building the three major passages of logistics, electricity and information in Latin America, enabling healthy interactions among the enterprises, society and government, and expanding the three financing channels of funds, credit loans and insurance) as well as a batch of major cooperation projects, including the representative transcontinental railway Brazil – Peru.

Connectivity is one of the 5 *Sectorial Axes* for the Community of Latin American and Caribbean States (CELAC). Against this backdrop, the *Integration of the Regional Infrastructure of South America (IIRSA)*, which is implemented by the Union of South American Nations (UNASUR), has experienced significant development and success. The integration of railways is a crucial component of the IIRSA, whose plans for railway reconstruction and development provide excellent opportunities for the cooperation of railway construction between China and countries in South America. Therefore, in consideration of the existent railway network in South America and plans for the integration of railways, China is supposed to be benefit from its cooperation in the construction of the Brazil – Peru Bioceanic Railway Corridor and thus to work with Southern American countries to carry out its railway network planning of "Four Horizontal and Two Vertical" (namely, four horizontal railways linking the Pacific and the Atlantic, two vertical railways running across the continent) and other cooperated construction in relation with the planning. Meanwhile, the planning should be in compliance with the basic cooperation principle of "bilateral and multilateral cooperation in parallel, flexible and voluntary participation".

I. Latin America Is a Natural Extension of the Belt and Road Initiative

The Maritime Silk Road linking China and Latin America across the Pacific was existent in the history. According to the experts, from 1567 to 1815, 108 manila galleons were sailing from the port of Acapulco (present – day Mexico) to Manila in the Philippines which were both part of New Spain, and the bulk of what these trading ships were carrying was China's raw silk and silk fabrics. Therefore, this trading route between Acapulco and Manila was called the Maritime Silk Road①. In the 21st century, the trade volume between China and Latin America has experienced substantial growth, driving the development of trade between East Asia, Southeast Asia and Latin America.

1.1 China – Latin American Trade Is the Engine Driving Trade between East Asia, Southeast Asia and Latin America

From 2000 to 2013, the total volume of import and export trade between China and Latin America increased from $ 12.6 billion to $261.4 billion, increased by $ 244.8 billion②; the total trade volume between East Asia, Southeast Asia and Latin America hit to $ 412.3 billion from $ 47.6 billion, increased by $364.7 billion③. During this period, the China – Latin America trade accounted for 68% of the growth of trade between East Asia, Southeast Asia and Latin America.

While Latin America stands on one side of the Pacific, East Asia and Southeast Asia across the ocean are major areas covered by the Belt and Road Initiative. Compared with Latin America, the two Asian areas have relatively abundant supply of labor and capital, whereas natural resources is inadequate by comparison. For this reason, goods imported from Latin America to East Asia and Southeast Asia are mainly primary products. During the period between 2000 and 2014, the value of imported goods from Latin America to East Asia and Southeast Asia, including China, reached to $ 155.3 billion from $ 12.4 billion among which imports of primary products jumped to $ 145.2 billion from $ 10.0 billion and the proportion grew to 93.5% from 80.9% (Table 1).

Importation demand for products of natural resources from Latin

① Le Jinming, "Maritime Silk Road Connect China – Latin America Trade" , *Maritime History Stndies*, no.2 (2001). Note: The Philippines was under the Spanish colonial rule from 1565 to 1898; Mexico was under the Spanish colonial period rule from 1519 to 1821. Mexico declared independence in 1810 and was officially recognized by Spain in 1821.

② Statistics from National Bureau of Statistics of China, http://data.stats.gov.cn, (accessed May 21, 2016).

③ Statistics from United Nations Conference on Trade and Development, http://unctadstat.unctad.org/wds/ReportFolders/reportFolders.aspx, (accessed March 16, 2016).

America to East Asia and Southeast Asia will continue to grow. China, for example, imported 50.65 million tons of soybean, 207.37 million tons of iron ore and its concentrate, 4.62 million tons of copper ore and its concentrate, and 39.46 million tons of crude oil from some Latin American countries in 2015①. Organization for Economic Co – operation and Development (OECD), CAF – Latin American Development Bank (CAF – Latin American Development Bank), United Nations Economic Commission for Latin America and the Caribbean (ECLAC, Spanish abbreviated as CEPAL) believe that China will import more agricultural products, minerals and crude oils from Latin America. As demonstrated in Table 2, from 2016 to 2020, the expected average growth rate per annum of China's import of agricultural products, minerals and crude oil from Latin America are 3.8%, 5.8% and 6.1% respectively; from 2021 to 2030, these number are expected to be 2.0%, 2.8% and 2.7%.

Table 1:
Imports from Latin America to East Asia and Southeast Asia in 2000 and 2014

	Value of Imports [(in) billion US dollars]		Primary Products [(in) billion US dollars]		Proportion of Primary Products (%)	
	2000	2014	2000	2014	2000	2014
China	4.78	109.36	4.22	104.71	88.3	95.7
East Asia and Southeast Asia (China Excluded)	7.61	45.94	5.80	40.49	76.2	88.1
Total	12.39	155.30	10.02	145.20	80.9	93.5

Source: Statistics from United Nations Conference on Trade and Development, http://unctadstat.unctad.org/wds/TableViewer/tableView.aspx (accessed May 21, 2016).

① Statistics from UN Comtrade Database of United Nations Conference on Trade and Development, http://comtrade.un.org/data/, (accessed March 16, 2016). Source and quantity of soybean imports: Brazil (40.92 million tons), Argentina (9.73 million tons); iron ore and its concentrate imports: Brazil (185.23 million tons), Chile (11.09 million tons), Peru (10.72 million tons), Mexico (180,000 tons), Argentina (150,000 tons); copper ore and its concentrate imports: Peru (2.86 million tons), Chile (1.01 million tons), Mexico (590,000 tons), Brazil (130,000 tons), Bolivia (30,000 tons); crude oil imports: Venezuela (16.01 million tons), Brazil (13.16 million tons), Colombia (8.87 million tons), Argentina (580,000 tons), Ecuador (540,000 tons), Mexico (300,000 tons).

Table 2:
Expectation of Average Growth Rate Per Annum of China's Import of Agricultural Products, Minerals and Crude Oil from Some Countries of Latin America

	Country	2016–2020	2021–2030
Agricultural Products	Brazil, Argentina, Guatemala, Honduras, Nicaragua, Paraguay, Uruguay	3.8	2.0
Minerals	Chile, Peru	5.8	2.8
Crude Oil	Bolivia, Colombia, Ecuador, Venezuela	6.1	2.7

Source: OECD/EALAC/CAF (2015), *Latin American Economic Outlook 2016: Towards a New Partnership with China*, p137, OECD Publishing, Paris.

1.2 China and Latin America Begin to Carry out All – round Cooperation in Infrastructure Construction

One of the bottlenecks that hinder the economic growth in Latin America is its inadequate infrastructure. According to Inter – American Development Bank, logistics costs in Latin America and the Caribbean (LAC) range from 18% to 35% of the final value of the products, compared to 8% in OECD countries. For small and medium – sized enterprises, this percentage can exceed 40%. If all countries in the region would improve their infrastructure to the average level of other middle – income countries, regional growth in Latin America would increase by an average of 2 percent a year.①

The demand for investment into the infrastructure construction in Latin America is huge. The CELAC *2020 Planning Agenda Proposal*, or *Propuesta Agenda 2020,* published in August 2015 set Infrastructure and Connectivity as one of the 5 hubs, targeting sectors in transport, energy,

① Santiago Levy Algazi, "Infraestructura, Logística y Conectividad:Uniendo a las Américas", Document for "II Cumbre Empresarial de las Américas: Tendiendo Puentes en las Américas: Integración Productiva para un Desarrollo Inclusivo", Ciudad de Panamá, Panamá, 8–10 de abril, 2015.

telecommunications, water and sanitation. [1]The agenda proposed to increase investment to 5.5% of annual regional GDP in the construction of infrastructure. Basing on the calculation that total GDP in 2014 in Latin America was $ 5.7 trillion[2], the proposed investment would amount to $ 300 billion per year. The CAF – Development Bank of Latin America holds that the region's annual investment in infrastructure should range from $ 250 billion to $ 300 billion, with $ 150 billion to $ 200 billion for new infrastructure and the rest $ 100 billion for the operation and maintenance of existing infrastructure.[3]

Infrastructure is a major part of the overall cooperation between China and Latin America. As the ECLAC pointed out, China's trade and investment is of significant importance for Latin America, particularly South America, but the inadequate infrastructure in the region is severely hampering its trade with China. To increase export to China, countries in Latin America should strengthen cooperation with China in infrastructure construction.[4] The First Ministerial Meeting of the China – CELAC Forum, held in Beijing in January 2015, adopted the China – Latin American and Caribbean Countries Cooperation Plan (2015—2019). The IV part (Infrastructure and Transportation) in the cooperation plan made it clear that China and Latin American countries would promote infrastructure development in areas such as transportation, ports, roads and warehouse facilities, business logistics, information and communications technologies, broadband, radio and TV, agriculture, energy and power, and housing and urban development. In May 2015, Premier Li Keqiang proposed the"3×3" model for capacity cooperation between China and Latin American countries during his visit to Latin America. The first "3" is to jointly build the three major passages of logistics, electricity and information in Latin America.

---

① CELAC, "Propuesta Agenda 2020", Ecuador, 2015. (The other four are Sectorial Axes are Reducing Poverty and Inequalities, Education, Science, Technology and Innovation, Environment and Climate Change and Financing for Development)

② Statistics from the CELAC:(http://estadisticas.cepal.org/cepalstat/WEB_CEPALSTAT/Portada.asp, October 2015

③ CAF, *IDEAL 2014: La Infraestructura en el Desarrollo de América Latina – Desarrollo empresarial en los mercados de infraestructura y servicios relacionados*, Corporación Andina de Fomento, 2015.

④ Commission for Latin America and the Caribbean (ECLAC), *Latin America and the Caribbean in the World Economy*, pp.14–16, Santiago, Chile, 2015.

2. The Initiative for the Integration of the Regional Infrastructure of South America (IIRSA)

South America's synergy with the Belt and Road Initiative enjoys a relatively good condition. On December 4, 2014, the South American Infrastructure and Planning Council (COSIPLAN)① of UNASUR② held its annual ministerial meeting in Montevideo, Uruguay, to discuss the work summary 2014 of the Initiative for the Integration of the Regional Infrastructure of South America (IIRSA) and to approve the work plan 2015. According to the work summary 2014, the IIRSA has confirmed 579 Integration Priority Projects by September, 2014. The total investment amounts to $ 163.3 billion, involving three major sectors in transport, energy and communications.③

2.1 The Ambitious Planning for Infrastructure Development

From August 31 to September 1, 2000, heads of state from 12 Southern American countries, including Argentina, Bolivia, Brazil, Chile, Colombia, Ecuador, Guyana, Paraguay, Peru, Suriname, Uruguay, Venezuela jointly proposed the Plan of Action for the Integration of Regional Infrastructure in South America④ in the jointly issued communiqué in Brasilia. In December the same year, ministers of 12 countries in charge of transport, energy, and communications held a

---

① The South American Infrastructure and Planning Council of UNASUR (Consejo Suramericano de Infraestructura y Planeamiento, abbreviated as COSIPLAN) was established in January 2009 under the UNASUR Constitutive Treaty.

② Union of South American Nations, or in Spanish Unión de Naciones Suramericanas, abbreviated as UNASUR. In May 2008, 12 South American countries, including Argentina, Bolivia, Brazil, Chile, Colombia, Ecuador, Guyana, Paraguay, Peru, Suriname, Uruguay and Venezuela, signed the UNASUR Constitutive Treaty, marking the formal establishment of the UNASUR. The headquarter of the UNASUR is located in Quito, the capital of Ecuador.

③ Foro Técnico IIRSA, Comité de Coordinación Técnica, *Cartera de Proyectos del COSIPLAN*, V Reunión Ordinaria del COSIPLAN, Montevideo, Uruguay, 4 de diciembre de 2014.

④ The Spanish name of the Plan of Action for the Integration of Regional Infrastructure in South America is Plan de Acción para la Integración de la Infraestructura Regional Suramericana.

ministerial meeting in the Montevideo, Uruguay's capital, formally putting forward the Initiative for the Integration of the Regional Infrastructure of South America (IIRSA)① and the 2000—2010 Action Plan.

The decade from 2000 to 2010 was the preparation phase for the IIRSA, and major tasks during this period included reaching a consensus on principles in guiding thoughts and work methods, confirming approach for new regional development plan, dividing the South America into 9 Integration and Development Hubs, primarily selecting more than 500 projects from three major sectors in transport, energy and communications, formulating the 2005—2010 South American Infrastructure Integration Initiative, confirming 31 Priority Projects, etc.

In 2011, the IIRSA proposed to include the South American Council of Infrastructure and Planning (COSIPLAN). As an important permanent body of the UNASUR, COSIPLAN is responsible for coordinating and implementing the integration of infrastructure in South America. Based on results of the work of the IIRSA from 2000 to 2010, the COSIPLAN formulated the Strategic Action Plan 2012—2022 and The South American Integration Priority Project Agenda (API)②.

As a major component of the COSIPLAN, the IIRSA is responsible for the formulation of the infrastructure integration program of South America, updating, evaluating and overseeing the implementation of integration projects, evaluating relative projects with reference to the principles of sustainable development of the economy and society, environmental protection, ecological balance, etc. Also, the IIRSA undertakes the responsibility to update, optimize or adjust project portfolio in accordance with the consensus reached at the annual ministerial meeting of the COSIPLAN, and would submit annual work summary and work plan of the next year to the COSIPLAN and so on.

The Inter – American Development Bank believes that the IIRSA is

① The Spanish name of the Initiative for the Integration of the Regional Infrastructure of South America is Iniciativa para la Integración de la Infraestructura Regional Suramericana, abbreviated as IIRSA. Website: www.iirsa.org.

② The Spanish names for the Strategic Action Plan 2012—2022 and The South American Integration Priority Project Agenda (API) are respectively Plan de Acción Estratégico 2012—2022 (PAE) and Agenda de Proyectos Prioritarios de Integración (API).

the most imaginative and dynamic initiative for regional infrastructure development undertaken in the Western Hemisphere ①. Total number of Priority Projects for infrastructure integration confirmed by the IIRSA for the period from 2007 to 2014 increased from 349 to 579. The estimated investment grew from $ 60.5 billion to $ 163.3 billion, and completed annual investment increased from $ 6.9 billion to $ 20.4 billion. By 2014, the number of Priority Projects completed has amounted to 106②.

Table 3:
Number of Priority Projects for Infrastructure Integration Confirmed by the IIRSA from 2007 To 2014

	Number of Projects	Estimated Investment [(in) $ billion]	Completed Investment [(in) $ billion]
2007	349	60.5	6.9
2008	514	69.0	10.2
2009	510	74.5	10.4
2010	524	96.1	14.0
2011	531	116.1	10.4
2012	544	130.1	12.7
2013	583	157.7	16.3
2014	579	163.3	20.4
2015	593	182.4	21.6

Sources: (1) IIRSA, *Agenda de Implementación Consensuada 2005–2010,* 2007, 2008, 2009, 2010.(2) COSIPLAN, IIRSA, *Informe de Actividades,* 2012,2013,2014.(3)COSIPLAN, IIRSA, " Cartera de Proyectos del COSIPLAN: Agenda de Proyectos Prioritarios de Integración (API)" ,Resultados del Trabajo de Actualización 2015 ,XXVII Reunión de Coordinadores Nacionales 19 de agosto de 2015, Montevideo.

2.2 The Organization of the IIRSA

The organization of the IIRSA includes the Coordinating Committee, Coordinating Committee on Financing, Working Groups and the

① Inter – American Development Bank, Initiative for the Integration of Regional Infrastructure in South America (IIRSA), *Building a New Continent: A Regional Approach to Strengthening South American Infrastructure*, Washington, D.C., 2006, Inter – American Development Bank.

② COSIPLAN, IIRSA, *Informe de Actividades*, 2012, 2013, 2014.

secretariat and other supporting bodies.

By the end of the 2014, the Coordinating Committee has had 28 National Coordinators. Bolivia, Colombia, Ecuador and Guyana respectively have 3 coordinators, and the rest 8 countries each have 2 coordinators. Coordinators from Argentina, Bolivia, Brazil, Colombia, Ecuador, Guyana, Paraguay, Peru, Suriname and Uruguay are officials of their respective country's government departments in development plans, infrastructure and public investment, while Coordinators from Chile and Venezuela are officials of Foreign Ministry of their respective countries. Coordinators of the Coordinating Committee meet once every two years to consider the implementation of the annual work plan of the IIRSA.

The Coordinating Committee has a number of working groups, which are respectively responsible for Integration and Development Hubs, Integration Priority Projects, prevention for risks and disasters, assessment of environmental and social impact, facilitation in border clearance, collection of geographic information and maps, financing mechanisms and guarantees, air integration, trade integration, logistics and production integration, territorial development integration, rail integration, telecommunications integration, information and network integration and other matters. Each working group has a country acting as coordinator. For instance, Brazil is the coordinator of the Working Group on Financing Mechanisms and Guarantees, and the coordinator of the Working Group on Rail Integration is Uruguay. The Working Group on Rail Integration was established in November 2011 and held its first working group meeting in September 2013 and held its second meeting in May 2014. The Working Group on Rail Integration is further sectored into a number of subgroups, such as Subgroup on the Paranaguá – Antofagasta Bioceanic Railway Corridor (Argentina – Brazil – Chile – Paraguay), which involves Chile, Argentina, Paraguay and Brazil, has completes the study on feasibility of the railway project. The Subgroup on the Central Bioceanic Railway Corridor (Bolivia – Brazil – Peru) will be active since 2015, and would carry out its study on the feasibility of its project.

The Coordinating Committee on Financing is composed of multilateral financial institutions such as the Inter – American Development Bank, the CAF – Latin America Development Bank and the La Prada Development

Fund (FONPLATA). The committee was set up to provide necessary finance and financial support for the Priority Projects confirmed by the IIRSA.

The Secretariat sets up its office in Buenos Aires, Argentina. The Secretariat works with the Inter – American Institute for Integration of Latin America and the Caribbean (INTAL) of the Inter – American Development Bank, which is responsible for day – to – day affairs.

2.3 Progress of the IIRSA Projects in 2014

Up to September 2014, the total 579 Integration Priority Projects primarily belong to three major sectors in transport, energy and communications. These projects involve①:

- 1 freight and passenger airport
- 6,245.23 km of roads
- 7 main bridges and 148 complementary bridges
- 2 bi – national tunnels and 20 complementary tunnels
- 2 beltways
- 7,342.4 km of rails
- 8,950.1 km of waterways in 14 rivers and 2 lakes
- 6 river ports
- 4 sea ports
- 6 logistic centers
- 13 border crossings
- 1,500 km trunk gas pipeline
- 2 500–kV transmission lines along 624 km

The IIRSA sets 10 Integration and Development Hubs in total, and they are: Andean Hub (AND), Peru – Brazil – Bolivia Hub (PBB), Paraguay – Paraná – Waterway Hub (HPP), Capricorn Hub (CAP), Guianese Shield Hub (GUY), Amazon Hub (AMA), Central Interoceanic Hub (IOC), MERCOSUR – Chile Hub (MCC), Southern Hub (DES) and Southern Andean Hub (ADS). The Priority Projects are mainly from the first 9 Hubs.

According to relevant reports and documents on the official website

① UNASUR, COSIPLAN, *Agenda de Proyectos Prioritarios de Integración: Informe de Avance 2014*, Montevideo, Uruguay, 4 de diciembre de 2014.

of the IIRSA①, the Andean Hub (AND) involves five countries (Bolivia, Colombia, Ecuador, Peru and Venezuela), featuring the plan to build two large north – south road corridors that connect the main cities of the five countries. As of October 2014, the Andean Hub has 64 API projects, and the total investment is estimated to be $ 10 billion, covering 2.6 million square kilometers and more than 100 million people within the area. GDP in the AND Hub is about $ 362 billion, 91.7% of which are mainly in Colombia and Venezuela.

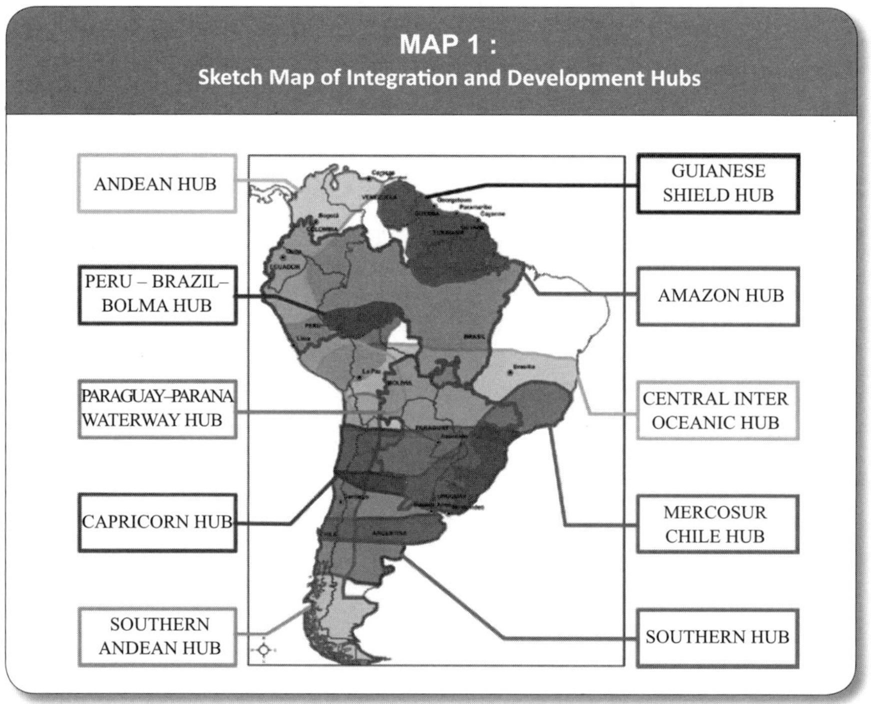

The Peru – Brazil – Bolivia Hub (PBB) is located at the junction

① UNASUR, COSIPLAN, *Cartera de Proyectos 2014*, Montevideo, Uruguay, 4 de diciembre de 2014.

UNASUR, COSIPLAN, *Agenda de Proyectos Prioritarios de Integración: Informe de Avance 2014*, Montevideo, Uruguay, 4 de diciembre de 2014.

IIRSA, Ejes de Integración y Desarrollo, www.iirsa.org (5 January, 2015)

ote: As a result of the overlap of the geographical scope of these Hubs, two API projects have been counted more than once, resulting in the calculation of 581 API projects of the nine Hubs in total, 2 more than the number in Table 3.

of the three countries. The PBB Hub has 25 API projects, and the total investment is estimated to be $ 32.1 billion, covering 1.1 million square kilometers and some 10.2 million people within the area. GDP in this is about $ 20.4 billion.

The Paraguay – Paraná – Waterway Hub (HPP) involves five countries (Argentina, Bolivia, Paraguay, Brazil and Uruguay), and has 95 API projects. The total investment in the HPP Hub is estimated to be $ 7.6 billion, covering 3.8 million square kilometers and about 73.2 million people within the area and some $ 420 billion of GDP.

The Capricorn Hub (CAP) is located between 20° south latitude and 30o latitude, and is an economic belt connecting the Pacific and the Atlantic. The CAP Hub involves Chile, Argentina, Paraguay, Uruguay and Brazil. It has 83 API Projects, with the estimated investment of 17.9 billion in total. The CAP Hub covers 2.8 million square kilometers and impacts the total population of about 50 million. GDP of the area is about $ 230 billion.

The Guianese Shield Hub (GUY) involves four countries (Brazil, Suriname, Guyana and Venezuela) and has 20 API projects, with the estimated investment of $ 10 billion in total. The GUY Hub covers 4 million square kilometers and some 24.5 million people within the area. GDP of the area is about $ 200 billion, 99.1% of which are mainly in Brazil and Venezuela.

The Amazon Hub (AMA) involves four countries (Brazil, Colombia, Ecuador and Peru) and focuses on building multimodal corridors linking the Pacific and the Atlantic with waterways of the Amazon Rivers as the main part. The AMA Hub has 82 API Projects, with the estimated investment of $ 25.1 billion in total. It covers 8.1 million square kilometers and some 120 million people within the area. GDP of the area is about $ 815 billion.

The Central Interoceanic Hub (IOC) is located between 12o south latitude and 22o latitude, and is an economic belt connecting the Pacific and the Atlantic. The IOC Hub involves Chile, Peru, Paraguay, Bolivia and Brazil. It has 61 API Projects, with the estimated investment of 8.9 billion in total. The IOC Hub covers 3.5 million square kilometers and impacts the total population of about 92.6 million. GDP of the area is about $ 486 billion, 94.6% of which are mainly in Brazil.

The MERCOSUR – Chile Hub (MCC) involves five countries (Chile, Argentina, Paraguay, Uruguay and Brazil) and has 123 API projects, with the estimated investment of $ 54.6 billion in total. The MCC Hub covers 3.2 million square kilometers and some 140 million people within the area. GDP of the area is about $ 850 billion, 88.3% of which are mainly in Brazil and Argentina.

The Southern Hub (DES) is located between 37o south latitude and 43o latitude, and is an economic belt connecting the Pacific and the Atlantic. The DES Hub involves Chile and Argentina. It has 28 API Projects, with the estimated investment of 2.7 billion in total. The DES Hub covers 500,000 square kilometers and impacts the total population of about 5.8 million. GDP of the area is about $ 35 billion.

According to the progress of these API Projects, by September 2014, 106 projects have been completed, and the completed investment has amounted to $ 20.4 billion. The number of API Projects in the execution is 179, with the estimated investment of $ 73 billion in total. The number of the API Projects in the phase of feasibility study of pre – execution is 157, and the investment is estimated to be $ 50.7 billion while Projects in the phase of pre – feasibility of pre – execution is 137, with the estimated investment of $ 19.2 billion.

The IIRSA has the following distinct characteristics:

First, the transport sector is the main focus. 89% of the API Projects (516) fall in the transportation sector, and the total investment for these Projects is about $ 108.6 billion, constituting 66.5% of all the estimated investment for API Projects. The number of API Projects in road transport subsector is 241, with the estimated investment of $ 56.3 billion. For rail subsector, the number of the Projects is 68, with the estimated investment of $ 32.8 billion. 54 API Projects are for the energy subsector, accounting for 9% of all, and the estimated investment for these 54 Projects is $ 54.7 billion with the proportion of 33.5% of the estimated investment in all.

Second, API Projects are exclusive national on the whole. Projects involving a single one country are national while projects involving two or more countries are multinational projects. 82.4% of all API Projects (477) are exclusively national and the rest 17.6% (102) are multinational. Argentina has the largest number of priority projects (180) among which

145 national Projects and 35 multilateral ones. The following country is Brazil (106), with 79 national Projects and 27 multinational ones. Concerning the investment, Brazil's investment is estimated to be about $ 79.1 billion and is the top one the list. The second biggest investor is Argentina, and the number is 43.9 billion. Meanwhile, Paraguay, Chile, Peru, Bolivia and other countries are all estimated to invest more than $ 10 billion.

Third, public investment is the main source of financing. In the sector of transport, 62.6% of the investment is public, 26.6% is private investment and 10.8% are public/private. These numbers in the energy sector are respectively 43.7%, 3.0% and 53.3%。 In communications sector, 95.2% of the investment comes from private source, with the rest 4.8% serving as public investment.

Fourth, establishing the four bioceanic corridors and the three economic belts are the main content of the API Projects. The Amazon Hub (AMA), the Peru – Brazil – Bolivia Hub (PBB), the Central Interoceanic Hub (IOC), the Capricorn Hub (CAP) and the MERCOSUR–Chile Hub (MCC) have 374 API Projects in total, accounting for 64.6% of the whole. The demanded investment for these Projects will be about $ 140 billion, taking up 85.7% of all estimated investment. These five Integration and Development Hubs has formulated four bioceanic corridors and three economic belts. The four bioceanic corridors are Valparaíso (Chile)–Buenos Aires (Argentina) Bioceanic Corridor, Paranaguá (Chile) – Antofagasta (Brazil) Bioceanic Railway Corridor, Peru – Bolivia – Brazil Bioceanic Corridor and Peru – Ecuador – Colombia – Brazil Multimodal Bioceanic Corridors. From the north to the south, the three major economic belts are: Peru, Ecuador, Colombia, Brazil Economic Belt with the development of the Amazon basin as the main target, Peru, Bolivia, Brazil Economic Belt with the main goal of developing the southern hinterland of the South American continent, and the Chile, Argentina, Paraguay, Uruguay, Brazil Economic Belt aiming to strengthen integration.

2.4 Major Difficulties and Challenges for the IIRSA

2015—2022 is an important period for the IIRSA to continue to progress, during which 63 priority projects are expected to be completed[①], such as the Port of Antofagasta (Chile) - Port of Paranaguá (Brazil) Bioceanic Railway Corridor API project that is going to be completed in 2019.

The advancement and implementation of the IIRSA are confronted with two major difficulties or challenges.

2.4.1 The first difficulty is the shortage of financing. Investment completed in 2014 accounted for only 12.5% of the total amount of estimated investment, leaving the funding gap of up to more than 140 billion dollars. Investment completed by Brazil in 2014 is approximately $ 7.37 billion, accounting for 9.3% of the total for all API Projects in the country, and the funding gap is roughly $ 71.1 billion. Argentina invested roughly $ 5.68 billion, completing 12.9% of the total and leaving a funding gap of $ 38.2 billion[②].

The Inter – American Development Bank (IDB) is the main source of financing for the IIRSA. Since 2000, the Inter – American Development Bank has been providing financing for the IIRSA. In the decade from 2000 to 2010, $ 2.9 billion of loans were issued by the IDB to support 28 API Projects, accounting for 28% of all investment in these Projects ($ 10.2 billion)[③].

In 2014, the Inter – American Development Bank (IDB), Development Bank of Latin America (CAF) and the Fondo Financiero para el Desarrollo de la Cuenca del Plata, or the Financial Fund for the Development of the River Plate Basin (FONPLATA) ratified loans for 9 API Projects, totaling $ 730 million. In the same year, the 3 financial institutions approved $ 320 million for 58 API Projects in support for the feasibility study of these Projects[④].

2.4.2 The other challenge the IIRSA is confronted with is coordination within member countries. The IIRSA has 12 member

① INTAL, “Avances en integración física en la UNASUR: V Reunión de Ministros del COSIPLAN”, Carta Mensual INTAL N 220 – diciembre 2014. Calculated according to the data in Gráfico 3.

② UNASUR, COSIPLAN, *Cartera de Proyectos 2014* , anexo 6a, Montevideo, Uruguay, 4 de diciembre de 2014.

③ Official site of the Inter – American Development Bank, www.iadb.org, (22 October, 2014).

④ UNASUR, COSIPLAN, *Cartera de Proyectos 2014* , anexo 6a, Montevideo, Uruguay, 4 de diciembre de 2014.

countries participating in its Projects, and because different countries has different conditions to consider, the IIRSA finds it difficult to make a relatively unified institutional arrangements in regional development projections, standards and approaches for screening API Projects, technical standards, evaluation regime for environmental and social impact, mechanisms in financing and guarantees. Meanwhile, owning to the high ecosystem diversity, South American countries are also facing pressures to protect the environment. In addition, some countries in the region are still in disputes over territories and borders, so there are also some obstacles in bilateral coordination and cooperation.

In July 2014, during the visit of Chinese President Xi Jinping to Latin America, China, Brazil and Peru jointly released a statement pledging concerted efforts to build a bioceanic railway corridor, and China will cooperate with the two countries carry out a feasibility study on the project, which is aimed at linking the Brazil and Peru. At the same time, the sector of infrastructure was also confirmed as one of the 6 cooperation priorities between China and Latin America. The IIRSA would be able to be a major platform for the cooperation in infrastructure between China and Latin America.

3. Railway Integration Is a Major Component of Infrastructure Integration in Latin America

Most of the Latin American countries attach great importance to railways, and some countries have formulated or are implementing their plans for railway rehabilitation and development. For now, the IIRSA has had 67 rail projects for an estimated investment higher than $47 billion[①].

3.1 Railways Has Played Significant Role in the Development of Latin American Countries

Most of the railways in Latin America were built before WWI (1914—1918). Cuba built the first railway in Latin America in

① http://www.iirsa.org/Page/Detail?menuItemId=101 (accessed June 18, 2016).

1837, which followed by Mexico, Brazil, Argentina and other Latin American countries who began to build extensive railways in the mid–19th century. By 1912, the total length of railways in Latin America has amounted to 100,000 kilometers, basically forming the railway network in the region. Building extensive railways played an important role in the economic growth and development of the Latin America. For example, railways generated 61.6%—84.2% of Brazil's GDP growth from 1864 to 1913, and the numbers for Mexico, Argentina and Uruguay are respectively 24.3% (1873—1910), 21.6 (1865—1913) and 8.4% (1874—1913).①

After 1950s, with the massive development of highways and roads, railways rapidly slipped out of its prime in road transportation, with many railway sections abandoned. The total length of railways in Latin America was 94,370 kilometers in 2007②, 5,000 kilometers shorter than that in 1912. Despite the fact, studies demonstrated that railways are still playing an important role in economic growth. Take Brazil as an example, during the period between 1950 and 1995, every 1% increase of investment in Brazil's railway construction could lead to 0.643% of Brazil's GDP growth, second only to electricity (0.683%) and much higher than telecommunication (0.428%) and motorways (0.399%)③.

3.2 The Existing Railway Network Are Mainly in South America

Railways in Latin America are mainly freight railways. As Table 4 demonstrated, up to 2012, the length of freight railways that are still in operation in Brazil, Argentina, Chile, Bolivia, Peru, Uruguay, Colombia, Venezuela, Paraguay and other countries in South America and Mexico, Panama adds up to 87,855 kilometers, of which Southern American countries take up 80% (69,995 kilometers). Mexico and Panama account

① Alfonso Herranz – Loncán, "Transport Technology and Economic Expansion: the Growth Contribution Of Railways in Latin America before 1914", *Revista de Historia Económica*, v.32, n.1, 2014.

② CEPAL, *Anuario Estadístico de América Latina y el Caribe 2013*.

③ Ferreira P.C., J.V. Issler, "Times Series Properties and Empirical Evidence of Growth and Infrastructure" , *Revista de Econometria*, v. 18, n.1, 1998.

for 20% (17,860 kilometers) in total.

Table 4:
Length of Freight Railways in Operation in 2012
(in) kilometers

Country	Rail Gauge(mm)					Total
	1000mm	1435mm	1600mm	1676mm	Mixed	
Brazil	22884		6687		523	30094
Argentina	7347	2704		18475		28526
Chile	1163			1991		3154
Bolivia	2438					2438
Peru	136	1738				1874
Uruguay		1641				1641
Colombia	1311	150				1461
Venezuela		804				804
Paraguay		3				3
Mexico		17787				17787
Panama		73				73
Total	35279	24900	6687	20466	523	87855

Note: Colombia's 1000mm rail gauge is practically 914mm.

Source: Asociación Latinoamericana de Ferrocarriles(ALAF, www.alaf.int.ar , accessed September 21, 2015).

Brazil has more than 30,000 kilometers of freight railways, boasting the longest freight railways in Latin America. Argentine follows Brazil and boasts 28,000 kilometers of freight railways. The third one is Mexico, with nearly 18,000 kilometers of railways for freights. In contrast, Panama and Paraguay respectively have only 73 and 3 kilometers of freight railways.

Unlike Mexico and Panama, the biggest feature for freight railways in South American countries is that they don't apply to the universal railway gauge. Mexico has its standard railway gauge of 1435mm, and the gauge of Panama's only one railway is 1435mm, too. Among South American countries, Bolivia, Uruguay, Venezuela and Paraguay have the same railway gauge, whereas Brazil, Argentina, Chile and Peru have two or three kinds of railway gauge. The meter gauge railway, which is relatively common, totals 35,000 kilometers and accounts for 50% of all freight railways in the South America, in which the practical gauge of the 1311 kilometers of meter gauge railways in Colombia is practically 914mm. Meter gauge railways are dominant of Brazil's freight railways, accounting for 76% of the total length (22,884 kilometers) in the country. Freight railways in Argentina, however, are mainly 1676mm – gauge railways, taking up 65% of the whole.

3.3 Historical Transcontinental Railways and Trans – Andean Railways Are Mostly Interrupted or Abandoned

There have been seven transcontinental railways and three Trans – Andean railways in the history of railway construction in Latin America. (Figure 2) Among the seven transcontinental railways, two are located in Mexico, three are in Central America (Guatemala, Costa Rica and Panama) and the rest two are in South America (Colombia, Chile, Argentina). Except for the two transcontinental railways in Mexico and Panama, the rest ones are all interrupted. The three Trans – Andean railways are either suspended or are very limited in freight capability.

3.3.1 Basic Facts of the Seven Transcontinental Railways

Mexico is bordered to the west by the Pacific Ocean and to the east by the Atlantic Ocean. Mexico has a relatively intensive railway network, thus it boasts several transcontinental railway corridors. There are two railways that were built relatively early and are of quite importance and use. One is the Manzanillo Port (Pacific coast) – Mexico City – Port of Veracruz (Atlantic coast) railway. With a total length of about 2,250 km, the railway was built in sections during the period between 1870 and 1910 and is still operating for now. The other one is the Port of Salina Cruz (Pacific coast) – Port of Mexico (Atlantic coast) railway. Opened to traffic in 1913, this railway is roughly 310 kilometers long, and some sections of the railway are still in operation currently.

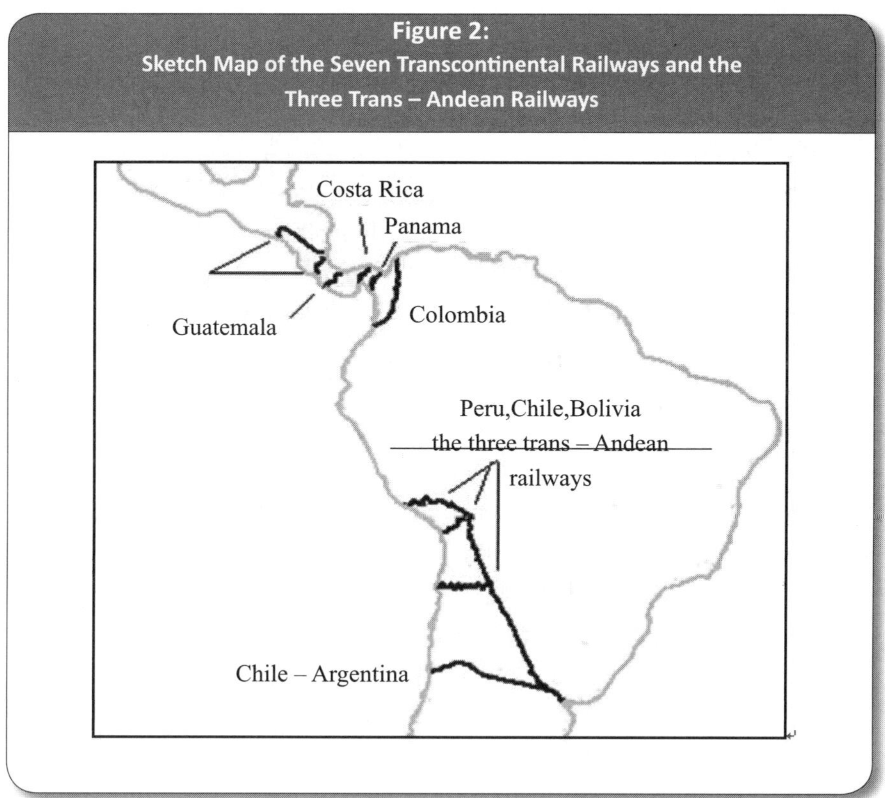

Figure 2:
Sketch Map of the Seven Transcontinental Railways and the Three Trans – Andean Railways

The Panama Railway was opened to traffic in 1855, and is the first transcontinental railways in America. The United States rebuilt the Panama Railway when it was building the Panama Canal from 1904 to 1912. The length of the railway is only 73 kilometers, thus becoming the shortest transcontinental railway in America. The maximum freight capacity of the railways is 2 million TEU (the volume of 20–foot – long container).

Costa Rica's Puntarenas Port (Pacific coast) – Limón Port (Atlantic coast) railway is the second transcontinental railway in Central America. With a total length of 300 kilometers, the railway was built in 1871, and was put into use entirely in 1890. The 7.5 Ms earthquake with Limón as the epicenter in 1991 and the hurricane in 1996 have interrupted the section of the San José (Costa Rica's capital) – Limón Port railway. So far it has not yet been restored.

Guatemala's Port of San José (Pacific coast) – Port of Puerto Barrios

(Atlantic Coast) railway is the third transcontinental railway in Central America. Built in 1892, the railway is toughly 725 kilometers in length and was opened to traffic in 1908. Currently, most parts of the railway are out of function.

Colombia's Port of Buenaventura (Pacific coast) – Port of Colombia (Atlantic coast) railway measures about 1400 kilometers, and was built in 1874, put into operation in 1930s. For now, most sections of the railway were abandoned, leaving only some 500 kilometers of it still in operation.

The Port of Valparaiso of Chile (Pacific coast) – Buenos Aires of Argentina (Atlantic coast) railway is the first transcontinental railway in South America. Construction of the 1430 kilometers – long railway was proposed in 1854, started in 1887 and completed in 1910. The railway's Los Andes (Chile) – Mendoza (Argentina) section is about 243 kilometers long, and was closed in 1984. Since 2004, Chile and Argentina have been planning to repair this section and are now in the preparation phase.

3.3.2 Basic Facts of the Three Trans – Andean Railways

The main purpose of building the three Trans – Andean railways is to open up a route for Bolivia's exports. From north to south, the three railways are:

(1) The Port of Mollendo (a Pacific port city of Peru) – La Paz (the capital of Bolivia) railway was opened to traffic in 1910. People on trains along this railway would travel from Mollendo to Puno (of Peru), then transfer ferries to get to Guaqui (Bolivia) across Lake Titicaca, and then get on trains again to La Paz. Currently, the Mollendo – Puno railway is still in operation while the Guaqui – La Paz section could only allow trains for tourism.

(2) The Port of Arica (Chile) – La Paz (the capital of Bolivia) railway was constructed in 1904 and opened to traffic in 1913. Total length of the railway is 440 kilometers, 207 kilometers of which is in Chile, and the rest 233 kilometers belongs to Bolivia. Interrupted in 2005, the section in Chile was repaired during the period between 2010 and 2012, whereas the Bolivia section is not restored yet.

(3) The Port of Antofagasta (Chile) – Oruro (Bolivia) railway was built in 1873 and began its service in 1888. The railway is 1537

kilometers long. Currently, the railway is still in operation, while is mainly for the copper ore transportation.

Across the Andes, the three railways could join railways in Argentina and stretch towards the Atlantic Ocean. However, on the direction towards the Brazil end, there is still no railway in the 24–kilometers distance between Bolivia's Port of Puerto Suárez and Brazil's Corumbá.

4. The "Four Horizontals and Two Verticals" Railway Network in South America Has Basically Formed

The South American Infrastructure and Planning Council of UNASUR (COSIPLAN) has set up the Working Group on Rail Integration, which is comprised of delegates from government departments of member countries. Taking the existing railway network and the need for economic and social development in the long run into consideration, the group is responsible for the formulation and planning on Rail Integration in South America and railway network within the framework of the IIRSA. Considering the bioceanic railways is the focus of Rail Integration in South America and the planning on railway network, the Working Group on Rail Integration set up the subgroup on bioceanic railways. The subgroup planned three bioceanic railways and one vertical railway (Three Horizontals and One Vertical). The Working Group on Rail Integration then combined the Three Horizontals and One Vertical, the Brazil – Peru bioceanic railway and Brazil's North – South Railway into the Four Horizontals and Two Verticals railway network in South America.

4.1 The Three Horizontals and One Vertical within the IIRSA Framework

The Three Horizontals refers to three east – west railways, namely the Port of Valparaiso (Chile) – Buenos Aires (Argentina) railway, the Port of Antofagasta (Chile) – Port of Paranaguá (Brazil) railway and the Peru – Bolivia – Brazil bioceanic railway. The One Vertical refers to a north – south railway, namely the Buenos Aires (Argentina) – Santa Cruz (Bolivia) railway.

4.1.1 The Port of Valparaiso (Chile) – Buenos Aires (Argentina) Railway

Rehabilitation of the Los Andes (Chile) – Mendoza (Argentina) section would connect the first transcontinental railway in South America. Governments of Chile and Argentina set the rehabilitation of the railway as one of the major projects in their bilateral cooperation, and jointly authorized the Entidad Binacional Túnel Las Leñas (Binational Entity Las Leñas Tunnel) to be responsible for the rehabilitation of Los Andes – Mendoza railway section. According to the feasibility study in August 2015, this section measures 204 kilometers, among which the length of tunnels is 52 kilometers, and the estimated investment would be $ 8.9 billion while the time for this rehabilitation would be 10 to 12 years. There are 3 rehabilitation and construction programs, namely the railway tunnel, Las Leñas tunnel and Agua Negra tunnel, and the three are called the bioceanic tunnels. The construction program for the Agua Negra tunnel has been confirmed basically: the total length of the tunnel is 13.9 kilometers while the altitude of the Argentine side is 4000–4800 meters and 3,600 meters above sea level on the Chilean side. The estimated cost is USD 1.4 billion, of which 28% will correspond to Chile and 72% to Argentina[①]. During the visit of Chinese Premier Li Keqiang to Chile in May 2015, Chilean President made it clear that Chinese companies are welcomed to participate in the construction of the bioceanic tunnels.

4.1.2 The Port of Antofagasta (Chile) – Port of Paranaguá (Brazil) Railway

The Port of Antofagasta (Chile) – Port of Paranaguá (Brazil) railway measures 3222 kilometers long and crosses Brazil, Argentina, Paraguay and Chile. The four countries have achieved consensus within the IIRSA framework, and plan to put the railway into operation in 2020. Based on the situation of operation and demand for building the railway, the line constructed would be separated into 7 sections.

The Antofagasta – Socompa (at the border of Argentina and Chile) railway is the only one section in Chile. The section is 370 kilometers

① Chile, "A ley tres protocolos que fortalecerán la conexión con Argentina"(www.iirsa.org ,11/08/2015).

long and will be operated by Chile's Antofagasta – Bolivia Railway Company.

Argentina has two sections of the railway. One is the 1467 kilometers – long Socompa – Resistencia section, which was operated by the Manuel Belgrano Railway Company and then was transferred franchise by the Argentine government to the Emepa Group. The other section is the Resistencia – Curuguaty (on the border of Argentina and Paraguay) railway. This section is the newly – built railway, and measures 60 kilometers.

Paraguay has one Curuguaty – Foz do Iguaçu section. The railway is 583 kilometers long and is also a newly – built railway. In June 2015, delegates from Brazil, Paraguay, Argentina and Chile of the subgroup on bioceanic railways held the second meeting on the Antofagasta – Paranaguá railway in Santa Cruz, Bolivia. Delegates of the subgroup reviewed and approved in principle the feasibility report on Curuguaty – Foz do Iguaçu railway worked out by Paraguayan government①.

There are 3 sections in Brazil. The first one is the Foz do Iguaçu – Cascavel railway. The railway is a new section and measures about 140 kilometers. The second one is Cascavel – Guarapuava section, which now has narrow gauge railway and measures 247 kilometers. The third one is Guarapuava – Port of Paranaguá (or Port of Sao Francisco do Sul) section. It is 355 meters long and has broad – gauge railway now.

4.1.3 The Peru – Bolivia – Brazil Bioceanic Railway

The Peru – Bolivia – Brazil Bioceanic Railway project was first proposed on the first meeting by the COSIPLAN Working Group on Rail Integration in September 2013. The report of the feasibility study was started to formulate in August 2015 and is scheduled to be completed by January 2016.

The construction of this railway can be described as Bolivia's "dream of a century". At the beginning of the twentieth century, with the opening of the three Trans – Andean railways, the problem of Bolivia's estuaries

---

① Subgrupo de Trabajo Corredor Bioceánico/COSIPLAN/UNASUR, "II Reunión Del Subgrupo De Trabajo Corredor Bioceánico Antofagasta – Paranaguá", Santa Cruz de la Sierra, 10 de junio de 2015.

was resolved, but the eastern and western railways in Bolivia needed to be connected in northern Argentina due to terrain factors. Since 1912, the Bolivian government has been actively commencing the construction of connecting Bolivian railways in the north and the south, namely the construction of the Cochabamba – Santa Cruz Railway. In the 1970s, with the support of the United States and Brazil, the Bolivian government conducted a preliminary study of the construction. Then from 2011 to 2014, with the support of the Inter – American Development Bank, the Bolivian Government conducted a feasibility study again.

According to existing research results, the Bolivian government will select the Port of Ilo as the railway's estuary to the Pacific Ocean. As the Port of Santos in Brazil is the railway's estuary to the Atlantic Ocean, the railway can be called the Ilo of Peru – Santos of Brazil Bioceanic railway. The Bioceanic railway is 3684 kilometers long.

From the Port of Iloilo in Peru to the east, the railway would pass Bolivia's La Paz, Oulu Luo, Cochabamba and Santa Cruz until finally arriving at Corumbá in Brazil. This section of the railway is about 1919 kilometers long, most of which are the new sections with relatively more bridge and tunnel constructions. The Corumbá – Port of Santos section measures 1765 kilometers and is a section of existing railway. Brazil's mining company plans to invest $ 6 billion to extend the line.

4.1.4 The Buenos Aires (Argentina) – Santa Cruz (Bolivia) Railway

The Buenos Aires (Argentina) – Santa Cruz (Bolivia) railway has been included into the program of Rail Integration in South America. The existing railway is entirely in operation, but the rail gauge in Argentina and Bolivia is different. The Belgrano railway in Argentina travels across the Buenos Aires – Rosario – Córdoba Argentina economic belt. In March 2015, Fondo Financiero para el Desarrollo de la Cuenca del Plata, or the Financial Fund for the Development of the River Plate Basin (FONPLATA) provided a $ 35 million loan to the Argentine government for the transformation and upgrading of the Belgrano Railway. The Bolivian section of the railway is the Eastern Bolivia railway, which is operated by Bolivia's Ferroviaria Oriental S.A., or Eastern Railway Company.

4.2 The Brazil – Peru Bioceanic Railway and the North – South Railway

In July 2014, during the visit of Chinese President Xi Jinping to Latin America, the three heads of state of China, Brazil and Peru jointly issued the Statement on the Cooperation between the Bioceanic Railways, proposing to set up a joint working group to carry out the basic study on the feasibility of the Brazil – Peru Bioceanic Railway. During the visit of Premier Li Keqiang in May 2015, the feasibility study of the Brazilian – Peru Bioceanic Railway was officially commenced. According to the website of Brazil's Federal Ministry of Transport, the feasibility study of the Brazilian section of this bioceanic railway will be completed in the first half of 2016, and its construction will be started in the second half of the same year.

The Brazilian section of the Brazil – Peru Bioceanic Railway and the North – South Railway are the two major railways in Brazil's railway development program during the period between 2012 and 2037. The two railways will constitute the "big cross" in Brazilian's railway network. The Brazilian section of the Brazil – Peru Bioceanic Railway is known as the Brazilian East – West Railway, whose east and west ends are respectively the Port of Campos and the border of Brazil and Peru. Since 2008, the Brazilian VALEC Engenharia, Construções e Ferrovias S.A., or Company of Engineering, Railways, and Construction (Valec) has conducted the feasibility study on the railway and the company estimated the investment would be approximately BRL 40 billion ($US 11 billion). Brazil's North – South Railway starts from the Rio Grande in southern Brazil, and travels to the north and until arriving at the Port of Belém near the mouth of Amazon River in the middle east of Brazil. The Valec company has franchise to build and operate the railway, and considering some sections are existing railways or have been finished, the company plans to complete the investment of BRL 22.6 billion (roughly $ 6.4 billion) for the North – South Railway during the period between 2015 and 2018.

4.3 The "Four Horizontals and Two Verticals" Railway Network in South America Has Basically Formed

IIRSA's Three Horizontals and One Vertical mentioned above, the

Brazil – Peru bioceanic railway and the North – South Railway could form the Four Horizontals and Two Verticals railway network (Figure 3).

4.3.1 The Four Horizontal refers to four east – west bioceanic railways. From north to south, they are:

(1) Brazil (Campos) – Peru (Bayovar) Bioceanic Railway

(2) Brazil (Santos) – Bolivia – Peru (Ilo) Bioceanic Railway

(3) Brazil (Paranaguá) – Paraguay – Argentina – Chile (Antofagasta) Bioceanic Railway

(4) Argentina (Buenos Aires) – Chile (Valparaiso) Bioceanic Railway

4.3.2 The Two Vertical refers to two north – south railways:

(1) Brazil's Rio Grande – Belém Railway

(2) Buenos Aires (Argentina) – Santa Cruz (Bolivia) Railway

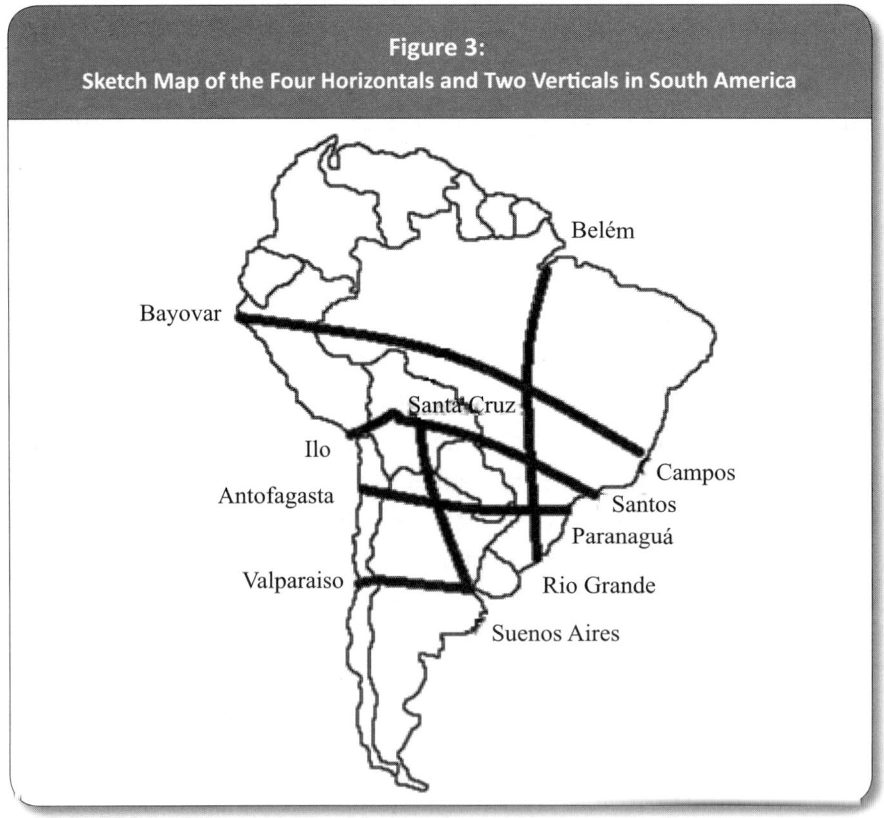

Figure 3:
Sketch Map of the Four Horizontals and Two Verticals in South America

5. The Proposal for China – South America Railway Cooperation Initiative on the Four Horizontals and Two Verticals Railway Network

The feasibility study on the Brazil – Peru Bioceanic Railway of China, Brazil and Peru is a signal that the railway planning and construction cooperation has been formally included into the agenda of China – Latin America cooperation. China has prepared financing for the China – Latin America cooperation on infrastructure cooperation, including railways, and proposed the China – South America Railway Cooperation Initiative basing on the Four Horizontals and Two Verticals Railway Network.

5.1 Improving Infrastructure Integration in South America Conforms to the Purposes of the Belt and Road Initiative

In March 2015, Chinese government officially published the *Vision and Actions on Jointly Building Silk Road Economic Belt and 21st – Century Maritime Silk Road (Vision and Actions on Belt and Road).* Although the document, which pointed out that "the Belt and Road run through the continents of Asia, Europe and Africa"①, did not include the Latin America, improving infrastructure integration worldwide is indeed the purpose of the Belt and Road Initiative.

Infrastructure integration is the material basis of economic globalization, while international rules and institutional arrangements of trade, investment and finance and others are the superstructure of economic globalization, thus both are vitally important. For so many developing countries (regions) all around the world, including South America, if their infrastructure, such as transportation, electricity and information, is relatively less integrated, then on international and domestic level, these countries will correspondingly benefit less from

① *Vision and Actions on Jointly Building Silk Road Economic Belt and 21st – Century Maritime Silk Road,* People's Daily, 04 edition, 29 March, 2015. Issued by the National Development and Reform Commission, Ministry of Foreign Affairs, and Ministry of Commerce of the People's Republic of China, with State Council authorization authorization.

international rules and institutional arrangements. In other words, improving infrastructure integration is one of the crucial prerequisites for developing countries (regions) to integrate into the process of economic globalization and to gain developmental benefits. History and practice have fully proved that even if those completely free trade agreements had been signed by those developing countries (regions), without the integration of infrastructure in line with the demand of these agreements, these agreements would not have too much significance and facilitation for the development of economies and societies of these countries.

The economic and social development of the developing countries (regions) is an important guarantee for the development of the global economy and the stability of the international community while the infrastructure is one of the main factors that promote the economic and social development of the developing countries (regions). Just as Santiago Levy Algazi, vice president of the Inter – American Development Bank, pointed out that "infrastructure is the main determinant of competitiveness. ①"Whether it is integration into the global production chain, or realization of inclusive growth and development in urban and rural integration, developing countries (regions) would need a lot of investment of infrastructure. Confronted with such a great demand for investment, the fact is that most developing countries do not have enough domestic savings, and government and private capabilities of investment are also relatively limited. Although existing multilateral financial institutions have made significant contributions, they are still far from meeting their demands.

5.2 Railways are the Focus of the Belt and Road Initiative and the IIRSA

With regard to Eurasia, Chinese government has expressed that China will actively participate and support the construction of the China –

① Santiago Levy Algazi, " Infraestructura, Logística y Conectividad:Uniendo a las Américas", Document for "II Cumbre Empresarial de las Américas: Tendiendo Puentes en las Américas: Integración Productiva para un Desarrollo Inclusivo", Ciudad de Panamá, Panamá, 8–10 de abril, 2015.

ASEAN Railway as early as in 2005. The railway travels across China, Myanmar, Laos, Vietnam and Singapore, and the total length of the railway is more than 14,000 kilometers. In September 2013, during his visit to Kazakhstan, Chinese President Xi Jinping put forward the strategic concept of the New Silk Road Economic Belt. As railway construction has been the focus since, the concept proposed to gradually form the transportation network connecting East Asia, Central Asia and Western Europe through building a railway corridor from the Pacific Ocean to the Baltic Sea. The railway construction is also the top priority of the Belt and Road Initiative. China's railway development plan has made it clear that the two railways in southern "Belt", namely the Yunnan – Burma Railway of the China – Myanmar – Bangladesh – India Economic Corridor and the China – Pakistan Railway of the China – Pakistan Economic Corridor. With regard to Africa, in May 2014, during the visit of Chinese Premier Li Keqiang to Kenya, China and Kenya signed the Cooperation Agreement on Mombasa – Nairobi Railway. The Mombasa – Nairobi Railway is the first new railway for Kenya in about a hundred of years, and is also the major support for Kenya to realize its *Kenya Vision 2030*. At the same time, the railway is also a major project for the connectivity in East Africa, which will connect Kenya, Tanzania, Uganda, Rwanda, Burundi and South Sudan, according to the long – term plan.

The TAZARA Railway in Africa is the first railway New China built overseas. The railway, which was stared to be built in October 1970 and was opened to traffic in July 1976, is seen as the monument for the brotherhood between China and Africa, even the third world countries. As mentioned above, railways are the focus of infrastructure integration in South America, and the Four Horizontals and Two Verticals railway network has basically formed. The railway cooperation between China and South American countries will spread China's railway construction comprehensively to Eurasia, Africa and Latin America, making railway the "steel bond" for the comprehensive construction and development of bilateral and multilateral economic and trade relations of China.

5.3 China's Financing to Support the Four Horizontals and Two Verticals Railway Network Construction in South America Is on the Increase

Since 2014, in order to support and promote the development of China – Latin American economic and trade cooperation, especially the China – Latin America overall cooperation, China has provided $ 70 billion in total, including the investment funds China unilaterally funded and unilateral loan commitments. On July 17, 2014 President Xi Jinping delivered a keynote speech entitled *Build a Community of Shared Destiny for Common Progress* when he attended the China – Latin American and Caribbean Countries Leaders Meeting in Brasilia, promising that China will launch the $20 billion special loan for infrastructure projects, $10 billion preferential loan to Latin American and Caribbean countries as well as $ 10 billion to launch the Fund for China – Latin America and the Caribbean Cooperation. On May 19, 2015, Premier Li Keqiang announced in the address at the closing ceremony of the China – Brazil Business Summit in Brasilia that China will set up a special fund for China – Latin America production capacity cooperation complete with $30 billion in support of relevant projects. In June 2015, Vice Premier Wang Yang of the State Council and then Vice President Michel Temer of Brazil jointly announced at the fourth meeting of China – Brazil High – level Coordination and Cooperation Committee that China will provide $ 15 billion for the $20 – billion fund to support production capacity cooperation between China and Brazil[①]. The financial resources China provided and promised to provide are far more than these funds, just as Table 5 demonstrates, the finance of merely the funds mentioned above has add up to $ 85 billion, which is in comparison with the $ 47 billion of the total 67 railway projects the IIRSA has already set up. Therefore, China has a relatively good financing basis for the railway cooperation with South American countries.

---

① Ministry of Commerce of the People 's Republic of China, Department of American and Ocean Affairs, *The fourth meeting of China – Brazil High – level Coordination and Cooperation Committee has been held successfully*, 30 June, 2015, (http://mds.mofcom.gov.cn/article/dzgg/201506/20150601029086.shtml) .

Table 5:
China's Financial Resources To Support Infrastructure Construction in South America

(in) $ billion

		Funds of China
Bilateral Financing Mechanism	China – Brazil Cooperation Fund on Capacity Production	150
Funds China Unilaterally Funds	Fund for China – Latin America and the Caribbean Cooperation	100
	Fund for China – Latin America production capacity cooperation	300
Unilateral Loans Commitments Made by China For Latin America	Special Loan for Infrastructure Projects in Latin America	200
	Preferential Loan to Latin America	100
Total		**850**

Sources: Information of the People's Bank of China, the Ministry of Foreign Affairs, the Ministry of Commerce and other government agencies as well as the official information reported by the Xinhua News Agency and other news organizations.

5.4 Basic Concepts of China – South America Railway Cooperation Initiative

5.4.1 Major policy papers, basic cooperation principles and main objectives. The major policy papers include *China – Latin American and Caribbean Countries Cooperation Plan (2015–2019)*, *Beijing Declaration*, *CELAC 2020 Planning Agenda Proposal*, *Integration of the Regional Infrastructure of South America (IIRSA)* and railway projects of the South American Infrastructure and Planning Council of UNASUR (COSIPLAN). The basic cooperation principle is "bilateral and multilateral cooperation in parallel, flexible and voluntary participation". The main objective is to the cooperation and development of highways, ports, airports, manufacturing, agriculture, mining and many other industries through the construction of railways.

5.4.2 Guiding approaches. The initiative should put reconstruction first while new construction second, freight lines first while passenger lines second, financing first while investment second. Most railways of the Four Horizontals and Two Verticals railway network are existing ones, thus only a small part of the railways are new construction projects. At the same time, as most sections of the railway network are still operating, so it would be enough to basically achieve the objective of the initiative with reconstructions or rehabilitations of certain sections.

5.4.3 Take bilateral cooperation as the principle while carrying out relative work separately. There are many plans and designs for railway construction in South America, such as the IIRSA, Brazil's planning of railway development, Paraguay's planning of railway construction, etc. As there might be a certain degree of difference or even conflict between different programs, in order to avoid unnecessary contradictions and disputes, it is recommended to separately carry out feasibility studies and planning while taking bilateral cooperation as the principle and focusing on cooperation objectives that have been reached.

5.4.4 Construction should be implemented in sections and phases. Considering that the national conditions vary widely and the relevant sections of railways in different countries are also different, construction should be implemented in sections and phases.

Report Four

A Case Study of Guangdong Base for Investigation of China's National Conditions: Economic and Trade Relations between Guangdong Province and Latin America

Yue Yunxia and Zheng Meng

Faced with continued sluggishness, the world economy has entered the new normal, with the growth of international trade markedly slowing and international investment going through ups and downs. China's economy has also entered the new normal. Foreign demand is no longer the main driving force of China's economic growth. Previously, the growth of China's investment, domestic or foreign, was based on the long – term growth of overseas market demand. As a result, China's excess capacity was exacerbated. Therefore, in a sense, international capacity cooperation is an integral part of the transformation and upgrading of the Chinese economy and it will lead the new normal of both the world economy and China's economy.

Under such circumstances, economic and trade relations between China and Latin America are still close, despite the long distance between them across the Pacific Ocean. Latin America demonstrates enormous potential because it is one of the major areas where many developing economies are concentrated. It is an important investment destination for Chinese companies. According to China's official statistics, China – Latin American trade volume reached \$ 236.5 billion in 2015. At present, China is Latin America's second largest trading partner and the third largest source of investment, and Latin America is China's seventh largest trading partner. From November 17 to 23, 2016, Chinese President Xi Jinping paid a state visit to Ecuador, Peru and Chile and attended the 24th APEC Economic Leaders' Meeting in Lima, Peru. Later, on November 24, the Chinese government released its second policy paper on Latin America and the Caribbean. President Xi has visited Latin America three times in his four – year tenure, which shows how important Latin America is for China. History has proved that the mutually beneficial cooperation between China and Latin America has great potential and that it is in line with the common interests of both sides and beneficial to the development and prosperity of the world. It epitomizes China's foreign cooperation, which should have a consistent approach in the framework of not only the Belt and Road Initiative but also the China – Latin America cooperation as a whole. Research on China – Latin America cooperation plays a prominent role in China's opening up strategy. It conforms to President Xi's basic opinions about global governance and building the global pattern.

In order to better understand the central government's strategy for China – Latin America cooperation and to provide targeted and practical policy recommendations for its implementation, in 2016, Guangdong Base for Investigation of China's National Conditions of the Institute of Latin American Studies of the CASS launched a new project—Research on Major Industries in Guangdong Province and Latin America—to explore the current situation, problems and participants' core demands in China – Latin America capacity cooperation in Guangdong Province. The research mainly covers the difficulties and challenges encountered and lessons learned by Chinese companies in their "going global", especially in the process of entering the Latin American market, and the policy demands of the central and local governments, as well as the role of the government, financial institutions, chambers of commerce and academic institutions in promoting the companies' "going global" and achieving comprehensive cooperation between China and Latin America. The research will further explore the meaning and principle of the new normal of Guangdong's economy. The findings can be transformed and used as a significant tool in helping Guangdong adapt to and even lead the new normal.

1. Research Objects and Research Process

As a pioneering province of reform and opening up, Guangdong entered the new normal earlier than other provinces. It is increasingly evident that Guangdong is taking the initiative to adapt to the new normal, and actively leading the new normal. Led by visionary leaders of the provincial party committee and provincial government, Guangdong speeds up the promotion of structural adjustment, transformation and upgrading and innovation – driven development, and implements "double transfer" (industrial transfer and labor transfer) and "double improve" (improve competitiveness and independent innovation capability). In this period, Guangdong's processing trade has witness a decrease in its speed and an increase in its quality and made a great leap forward with its technology and capital – intensive industry and a production mode that features commissioned design and independent brand; companies' "going global" has played a positive role for Guangdong in expanding international market, optimizing capacity allocation, gaining access to overseas production factor resources, enhancing the level of research and development technology and participating in international competition and cooperation; the private sector has gained a clear advantage with enhanced quality and efficiency and rapid innovation. Guangdong's independent innovation and industrial competitiveness has been in the rising. At present, there are six major trends, including the industrial differentiation, the innovative development of the processing trade, the leading development of the private sector, the change of capital organic composition, the high growth of productive service industry and the acceleration of "going global".

Guangdong is among the provinces that opened first to the outside world. It is the starting point of the Maritime Silk Road. It is also an important strategic hub, economic and trade cooperation center and an important engine under the Belt and Road Initiative. At the same time, due to its unique history, Guangdong has extensive economic and cultural exchanges with Macau, which is adjacent to Guangdong, and Portuguese – speaking countries, including Brazil. Guangdong companies, with unique characteristics, play a leading role in developing the Latin American market. Their lessons and experience are typical in China.

In the new economic cooperation framework of "1+3+6" initiated by President Xi, "1" means one plan, which refers to clarifying the common problems faced by China – Latin America cooperation, setting common goals and shared visions, and establishing a joint cooperation strategy on the basis of the strategic docking between China and Latin America; "3" means three major driving forces of the comprehensive development of China – Latin America cooperation, namely, trade, investment, finance; "6" means six key areas of China – Latin America cooperation, including energy resources, infrastructure construction, agriculture, manufacturing, scientific and technological innovation and information technology, with an aim of promoting the industrial docking between China and Latin America and deepening economic cooperation. Given the three driving forces in the framework, Guangdong province is chosen as the research object for this year, since its manufacturing industry develops better and it opened to the outside world early.

From July 17 to 21, 2016, the Institute of Latin American Studies of the CASS sent a research team, which was formed by the project teams of Research on Latin American Industry, economic subjects and Investigation of China's National Conditions, to Guangdong to research into the government, universities, think tanks, companies and many other units. The main purpose was to provide policy recommendations for better implementing the cooperation proposal put forward by President Xi in the 1st China – CELAC Forum ministerial meeting and to provide theoretical and decision support for achieving the two ten – year goals of China – Latin America trade and investment under new circumstances.

The main research objects included the government, universities, think tanks and companies (involving labor – intensive and technology – intensive industries). As to companies, the research focused on the difficulties and challenges encountered and lessons learned by Chinese companies in their "going global", and the policy demands of the central and local governments, as well as the role of the government, as well as the achievements and doubts of universities and think tanks in promoting the companies' "going global". At the same time, this research laid a foundation for future work. First, among the different stakeholders chosen as research objects, universities and think tanks already have sufficient research experience in the development of China – Latin

America relations. Second, only better – managed Chinese companies in the Latin American market were chosen as research objects, which provide rich experience in promoting the China – Latin America industry docking and economic and trade cooperation.

2. Guangdong Economic Development and Foreign Economic and Trade Cooperation

2.1 An Overview of Economic Development

Guangdong's economic aggregate ranks the first in China. Its economic growth has played an important supporting role in the national economic growth. Over the past five years, it contributed over 10% of the national economic growth rate. In the Twelfth Five – Year Plan period, Guangdong's economic aggregate grew steadily, reaching 5 trillion Yuan in 2011, exceeding 6 trillion Yuan in 2013. In 2015, it surpassed the 7 trillion Yuan mark, at 7.28 trillion Yuan, accounting for about one – tenth of that of the entire country. It is the 27th consecutive year that Guangdong's economic aggregate ranked the first nationwide since 1989. Per capita GDP exceeded US$10,000. With the sustained and rapid economic development, Guangdong's per capita GDP steadily increased. From 2011 to 2015, Guangdong's per capita GDP grew by 7.5% each year, which was 7% faster than the goal set in the Twelfth Five – Year Plan. In 2014, it increased by 7.1% at 63,469 Yuan, or US$10332, breaking the US$10,000 mark. In 2015, it reached US$10,800. In accordance with the income group thresholds established by the World Bank, Guangdong has reached the upper – middle income group level, close to the high income group level.

In the same period, the quality and industrial structure of Guangdong's industrial economy were actively improved. Three major industries formed the "Third Second First" structure. During the period of the Twelfth Five – Year Plan, agricultural development remained stable and industrial development declined. With the improvement of economic development, the demand for productive and living services was increasing. The constantly rising service industry became the largest industry in Guangdong. In 2013, the proportion of the added value at current price of the tertiary industry in Guangdong's GDP rose to 48.8%, exceeding the secondary industry as the largest industry of the national economy, thereby realizing the goal of the 12th Five – Year Plan two years earlier than scheduled. In 2015, the "Third Second First" structure was basically formed and the structure of the three industries became 4.6: 44.8: 50.6, with the proportion of the tertiary industry exceeding 50% for the first time at 50.6%.

Guangdong actively promoted the advanced manufacturing industry and modern service industry at the same time, maintained sustained and rapid economic development, achieved the optimization and adjustment of its economic structure, and significantly enhanced the potential and endogenous power of its economy. In the five years, the optimization and adjustment of Guangdong's economic structure were mainly reflected in two aspects—the internal upgrading of industry and the development of the service industry both picked up speed. Industrial transformation and upgrading gathered speed and evolved towards high – end directions. The development of strategic emerging industries was vigorously promoted. Electronics, equipment manufacturing, petrochemical industry and other industries further improved their industrial distribution and technologies. The advanced manufacturing and high – tech manufacturing industry grew faster than the overall industry and played leading roles. In Guangdong's enterprises above designated size, the proportion of the advanced manufacturing industry's added value increased from 47.0% in 2010 to 47.9% in 2015 and that of high – tech manufacturing increased from 21.1% in 2010 to 25.6% in 2015. The internal structure of the service industry was constantly optimized. While the traditional service industry maintained steady development, the modern service industry developed rapidly. In 2011, the modern service industry developed rapidly, with the financial services maintaining an average annual growth rate of 13.2%, scientific research and technical services 15.4%, and health services 14.7%.

Other services except cultural creativity and design services all had an average annual growth rate of more than 10%, such as the modern logistics industry, emerging information technology services, real estate leasing and business services.

In the Twelfth Five – Year Plan period, Guangdong Province implemented a new round of high – level opening up and speeded up the construction of a new system of open economy, so as to win the initiative in development and international competition, effectively resolve the international financial crisis, and further expand the depth and breadth of opening up.

The scale of import and export trade steadily expands. Despite the faltering world economic recovery since the international financial crisis, Guangdong's import and export trade has maintained a steady overall growth. In 2015, the total volume of imports and exports in Guangdong ranked first in the country at US$1.02 trillion, rising by 30.3% from 2010, an average annual increase of 5.4%. The total volume of imports and exports accounted for 25.9% of China's total trade volume. The import and export structure is optimized. As to different forms of trade, ordinary trade accounted for 34.2% of the total volume of imports and exports and increased to 42.1% in 2015; the proportion of processing trade dropped from 56.9% in 2010 to 43.0% in 2015; ordinary trade export accounted for 42.9% of Guangdong's total export in 2015. Processing trade companies accelerated the pace of transformation and upgrading. The export of "Commissioned Design plus Independent Brand" goods increased to 70% of the total export volume. Trading partners become more diversified. The relationship with the three traditional trading partners, namely the United States, Europe and Hong Kong, is consolidated. Meanwhile, trade with the emerging market countries develops quickly. Recently, Guangdong's trade with countries along "the Belt and Road" has been generally better than its overall trade. As to trading bodies, foreign – invested companies and private companies are the main forces of import and export in Guangdong. In 2005, the import and export of foreign – invested companies amounted to US$542.7 billion, accounting for 53.06% of the total import and export volume of the province. That of private enterprises was US $ 351.9 billion, accounting for 34.4% of the province's total. That of state – owned companies and collective companies accounted for 7.8% and 2.3% respectively, at US$79.9 billion and US$23.7 billion. As to trading regions, Asia recently has been the biggest trading region of Guangdong Province, followed by North America and Europe. In comparison, the trade volume in Latin America and Africa is lower. As to trading products, Guangdong mainly exports mechanical and electrical products, high – tech products such as automatic data – processing equipment and its components, hand – held or car wireless phones, clothing, textiles, furniture and other traditional labor – intensive products and imports mechanical and electrical products, high – tech products, ore, crude oil, plastic, steel, copper and unwrought copper.

Table 1:
Guangdong's foreign trade in different regions

	2010		2013		2014		2015	
Regions	Amount	Proportion (%)	Amount	Proportion (%)	Amount	Proportion (%)	Amount	Proportion (%)
Total Export	4531.91	100.0	6363.64	100.0	6460.87	100.0	6434.68	100.0
Asia	2504.24	55.3	4030.30	63.3	3887.16	60.2	3690.98	57.4
Africa	120.58	2.7	156.67	2.5	217.21	3.4	267.13	4.2
Europe	741.72	16.4	813.01	12.8	903.49	14.0	918.02	14.3
Latin America	203.46	4.5	272.58	4.3	286.57	4.4	303.37	4.7
North America	894.62	19.7	1003.77	15.8	1068.56	16.5	1151.00	17.9
Oceania & Other Regions	67.29	1.5	87.31	1.4	97.86	1.5	104.18	1.6
Total Import	**3317.05**	**100.0**	**4554.58**	**100.0**	**4304.97**	**100.0**	**3793.28**	**100.0**
Asia	2610.49	78.7	3425.76	75.2	3249.21	75.5	2955.25	77.9
Africa	61.52	1.9	291.27	6.4	276.09	6.4	165.24	4.4
Europe	300.21	9.1	344.10	7.6	346.56	8.1	292.92	7.7
Latin America	95.29	2.9	102.03	2.2	103.45	2.4	82.35	2.2
North America	169.96	5.1	282.12	6.2	246.47	5.7	229.70	6.1
Oceania & Other Regions	79.59	2.4	109.29	2.4	81.05	1.9	67.82	1.8

Source: Guangdong Statistical Yearbook in 2016.

Trade in services has made great progress. In 2015, the total imports and exports of services reached US$131.73 billion, an increase of 18.5%

year on year. From 2011 to 2015, the average annual growth rate was 20.9%. Service trade structure is gradually optimized. The export of computer, insurance, finance, consulting and other high value – added trade in services is gaining strong momentum.

Foreign capital is utilized to maintain steady growth. Guangdong used to focus on increasing the amount of foreign capital. Now attention shifts to improving quality. From 2011 to 2015, Guangdong's actually utilized FDI amounted to US$124.046 billion, with an average annual increase rate of 5.8%. Among Guangdong's actually utilized FDI, newly – signed FDI projects amounted to 7029, an increase of 16.8% than the previous year; the volume of contractual FDI reached US$561.1 billion, a rise of 30.3% than the previous year; actually utilized FDI was US$26.875 billion, up 0.01%.

It is increasingly apparent that FDI is flowing to high – tech industries, services (especially finance, insurance, livelihood and other services). In 2015, 56.9% of FDI were used in the tertiary industry, 17.6% higher than 2010. Non – financial direct investment grew rapidly, from US$3.53 billion in 2011 to US$10.56 billion in 2015, an increase of 51 times, with an average annual growth rate of 23.8%.

In terms of FDI, Guangdong's unprecedented achievements in international capacity cooperation made 2015 a milestone year of Guangdong companies' "going global". The FDI grew US$ 25.95 billion, up 104.9%. The actual investment was US$10.65 billion, a rise of 10.9%. The actual investment in manufacturing industry increased 1.6 times and that in the electrical manufacturing industry rose 11 times.

Huawei, Gree, Midea, Hytera, BYD, ZTE, Agribusiness, Rising, Yudean and other private companies have become Guangdong's international business leaders due to their transnational operation. Furthermore, Huawei and ZTE can be rated as world – class communications companies. According to statistics, private companies accounted for 90% of foreign investment. By the end of 2015, Guangdong had a total of 6492 overseas companies in 19 industrial categories throughout the world's 129 countries (regions) and the stock of foreign investment reached US$60.12 billion. By the end of 2014, the total assets of overseas companies reached US$530.27 billion. Asia, the main destination of investment, attracted 70% of investment.

Service, wholesale and retail, the two main industries, attracted 60% of investment. Investment forms shift from overseas trading companies to a series of other forms, including direct investment, equity replacement, cross – border mergers and acquisitions. The roles of Guangdong's overseas investment in the industry chain changed gradually from participants to leaders.

Guangdong is also at the forefront of China's foreign economic cooperation. With the implementation of the "going global" strategy gathering speed, the turnover of contracted projects in 2015 reached US$19.88 billion, an increase of 142.2% than 2010. The average annual growth rate from 2011to 2015 was 19.4%. Free trade area construction has made an important breakthrough. In 2015, Guangdong Free Trade Experimental Zone was formally established, including three areas, namely Nansha, Qianhai and Hengqin. Guangdong has been participating in the Belt and Road initiative cooperation, capacity cooperation and equipment manufacturing cooperation in a more active manner, promoting the construction of the international logistics channel and strengthening economic and trade cooperation with the countries along the "Belt and Road".

2.2 Conditions of the Cities Being Researched

2.2.1 Guangzhou

In 2015, Guangzhou's GDP was 1.810041 trillion Yuan, an increase of 8.4% year on year, which is higher than that of China (6.9%) and Guangdong (8.0%). The first, second and third industries' added value reached 22.809 100 billion Yuan, 578.621 billion Yuan and 1208.611 billion Yuan, a rise of 2.5%, 6.8% and 9.5% respectively. The industrial structure was more optimized and the structure of the three industries became 1.26: 31.97: 66.77. The proportion of the tertiary industry increased by 1.55% than the previous year (65.22%). Its contribution to the economic growth exceeded 70% for the first time at 70.6%.

In 2015, Guangzhou's total import and export was 830.641 billion Yuan, up 3.5% over the previous year (138.87 billion US dollars, up 2.5% over the previous year). The total exports were 503.467 billion Yuan, up 12.7%; the total imports were 327.774 billion Yuan, down 8.0%. The gap between imports and exports (exports minus imports) was 172.693 billion Yuan, an increase of 85.043 billion Yuan. Newly – signed FDI projects amounted to 1429, an increase of 23.7% over the previous year. Contractual foreign investment was 8.363 billion US dollars, an increase of 4.0%. The actually utilized FDI amounted to 5.416 billion US dollars, a rise of 6.1%. The amount of approved foreign investment agreement reached 5.133 billion US dollars, up 57.9% over the previous year. The turnover of foreign contracted projects and foreign labor service cooperation reached 855 million US dollars, up 49.6% over the previous year. By the end of the year, those who worked abroad for the contracted projects and labor service cooperation totaled 24,400.

2.2.2 Dongguan

In 2015, Dongguan's GDP was 627.56 billion Yuan, an increase of 8.0% year on year at comparable prices. The growth rate increased by 0.1% than the previous three quarters. The added value of the first industry was 2.05 billion Yuan, decreased by 0.4%; that of the second industry 290.298 billion Yuan, up 6.2%; that of the tertiary industry 335.159 billion Yuan, an increase of 10.0%. The industrial structure has been optimized. During the Twelfth Five – Year Plan period, in 2011 Dongguan's first, second, and third industry were in the proportion 0.4:51.2:48.4, forming a "Second Third First" structure, with industry playing the leading role; in 2015, the proportion became 0.3:46.3:53.4, forming a "Third Second First" structure, with services being the leader.

In 2015, the total volume of imports and exports was 167.673 billion US dollars (1040.776 billion Yuan, an increase of 4.2%), a rise of 3.1% than the previous year. Imports amounted to 63,955 million US dollars (397.246 billion Yuan, a decrease of 1.3%), deceasing 2.4%; exports 103.719 billion US dollars (643.53 billion Yuan, up 7.9%), up 6.9%. As to regions for exports, exports to Asia were 54.085 billion US dollars, increasing 4.7%; exports to North America 26.131 billion US dollars, increasing 10.1%; exports to Europe 16.91 billion US dollars, increasing 6.2%; exports to Latin America 3.427 billion US dollars, increasing 6.9% ; exports to Oceania 1.374 billion US dollars, an increase of 2.9%. Exports of electromechanical products were 70.712 billion US dollars, up 1.6%, accounting for 68.2% of total exports. Exports of high – tech products were 35.434 billion US dollars, decreasing 3.0%, making up 34.2% of the total. In the whole year, 440 new FDI projects were signed, and the amount of contractual foreign investment was 5,059 million US dollars, up 17.2%. The actually utilized foreign capital was 5.32 billion US dollars, an increase of 17.5%. Among it, the actually utilized foreign capital in communications equipment, computers and other electronic equipment manufacturing industry was 661 million US dollars, decreasing 26.6%. That in special equipment manufacturing industry was 247 million US dollars, increasing 4.0%.

2.2.3 Shenzhen

In 2015, Shenzhen's GDP reached 1750.299 billion Yuan, increasing 8.9% at comparable prices than 2014. The rate of increase in Shenzhen was 2.0% and 0.9% higher than that in China and Guangdong province respectively. In terms of the three industries, the added value of the first industry was 566 million Yuan, decreasing 1.7%; that of the second industry 720.553 billion Yuan, an increase of 7.3%; that of the tertiary industry 1029.18 billion Yuan, increasing 10.2%.

In 2015, the volume of total imports and exports in foreign trade was 2751.658 billion Yuan, down 8.2% from the previous year. Exports reached 1641.539 billion Yuan, down 6.0%, accounting for 11.6% and 41.1% of that in the country and Guangdong Province respectively. Imports reached 1110.191 billion Yuan, down 11.1%. The total amount of exports has ranked first among mainland cities for twenty – three consecutive years. The number of newly – signed FDI projects was 3,359, an increase of 34.9% over the previous year. The contractual foreign investment totaled 25.595 billion US dollars, up 134.9%. The actually utilized FDI was 6.497 billion US dollars, up 11.9%. The turnover of foreign contracted projects was 17.948 billion US dollars, up 74.7% over 2014.

3. Evolution of Industrial Structure in Guangdong

In recent years, accelerating industrial transformation and upgrading has been the main theme of Guangdong's economic development. Industrial transformation and upgrading is essential for transforming

Guangdong's overall economic development mode. Guangdong, as an important manufacturing base of China, attaches great importance to innovation – driven development. A series of new policies and new initiatives have been introduced to speed up the construction of a regional innovation system, strengthen production – study – research cooperation among ministries, provinces and academies, promote the research and commercialization of core technologies in intelligent manufacturing and push industries to the high end of the global industrial chain and value chain. At present, Guangdong has entered the key stage of innovation – driven development, transformation and upgrading. The fifth Plenary Session of the 18th CPC Central Committee put forward the concept of innovation, emphasized putting innovation at the core position in China's development as a whole, clearly pointed out the implementation of intelligent manufacturing projects and the establishment of a new industrial system, thereby providing a new direction and impetus for Guangdong's development.

3.1 Industrial Restructuring Process

Industrial restructuring is an important part of economic development. Guangdong's industrial development, industrialization process and the changes of high – growth industries in different periods have taken a 'catch – up' economic growth path that features a shift from light industry to heavy chemical industry to high processing industry. Since the reform and opening up, Guangdong's industrial restructuring has gone through three stages:

Stage One: Focusing on foreign technology and industrial development (1980–1997). From the start of Reform and Opening up to 1997, Guangdong formed an export – oriented economy through attracting foreign investment mainly with foreign technology. In the 1980s, Guangdong adopted a light and export – oriented industrial development strategy. Because of the Reform and Opening up policy and the advantages of being adjacent to Hong Kong and Macao, Guangdong adopted the approach of "three – processing and one compensation" and the mode of "having stores in front and factories behind", developed low – tech labor – intensive industries such as textile, clothing and daily necessities, thereby speeding up the industrialization process in Guangdong. In the 1990s, traditional manufacturing and electronic industries from Taiwan were transferred by means of the combination of investment and OEM production. The transferred industries were mainly high – tech industries like electronic information and home appliance manufacturing. They were transferred to Shenzhen, Dongguan and other places in the Pearl River Delta. Domestic demand began to shift from light consumer goods to durable consumer goods, contributing to the development of heavy industry. From 1991 to 2000, the average annual growth of heavy industry increased by 28.5%, 6% higher than that of light industry.

Stage Two: Focusing on independent innovation and technological breakthroughs (1998–2004). The financial crisis in Southeast Asia in 1997 had a great impact on Guangdong's economic growth. In order to solve the problem of insufficient demand, a series of policies and measures to expand domestic demand and promote export were introduced by the central and local governments in 1998. Guangdong facilitated its economic development by taking full advantage of the opportunity of Hong Kong reunification and the close relationship between Guangdong and Hong Kong. In 1998, the Guangdong Provincial Party Committee and the government promulgated the Decision on Promoting the Upgrading of *Industrial Structure through Scientific and Technological Progress*, put forward the strategy of invigorating Guangdong through science and education and promoted the strategic adjustment of economic structure and economic growth mode. Since the beginning of 2000, heavy industry has maintained a strong growth momentum. Heavy chemical industry with large income elasticity and high productivity benchmarks has become the main driving force of economic growth. The annual growth rate of heavy industry is 10% higher than that of light industry. Heavy industry are mainly technology – intensive industries and electromechanical industry that requires deep processing, including in particular electronics and communications equipment manufacturing, transportation equipment manufacturing, chemical raw materials and products industry, warehousing, post and telecommunications, wholesale and retail trade, catering and other industries.

Stage Three: Focusing on optimizing space and shaping the environment for innovation (2005 to the present). On March 7, 2005, the Guangdong Provincial Party Committee and the Guangdong Provincial Government promulgated *Opinions on Joint Promotion of Industry Transfer in Mountainous Areas, East and West Wings and Pearl River Delta* and *Special Plan for Economic Development of East and West Wings*, which help promote the Mountainous Areas and East and West Wings to accept the industrial transfer from the Pearl River Delta. In December 2007, the Second Plenary Session of the Seventh Central Committee of the Communist Party of Guangdong Province made a clear proposal to further emancipate the mind, change the economic development mode, and realize scientific development in Guangdong. The session analyzed comprehensively the five major deficiencies in the development of Guangdong in the context of globalization. The key problem is that, despite the large economic aggregate, the development model is still extensive, the economic structure and the ability of independent innovation is yet to be improved; the traditional development model that features large investment, high consumption, severe pollution and low efficiency has not been fundamentally changed; industrial competitiveness as well as core technologies and key technologies are limited. In May 2008, the Guangdong Provincial Party Committee and the Guangdong Provincial Government issued *Decisions on Promoting Industrial Transfer and Labor Transfer* and seven supporting documents, which are conducive to clearing the bottlenecks of industrial economic development in Guangdong, adjusting the layout of productivity, accelerating industrial restructuring, speeding up industrialization and urbanization, and promoting a new round of development. On June 19, the Guangdong Provincial Party Committee and the Guangdong Provincial Government issued *Decisions on Volunteering for Practice of Scientific Development*, and put forward the establishment of a modern industrial system that connects to the world and have distinct Guangdong features. On July 2, *Decisions on Speeding up Construction of Modern Industrial System* was issued to point out that the overall structure of the construction of modern industrial system is to develop six major industries, with modern services and advanced manufacturing being the core, and that Guangdong should build the eight major carriers of the modern industrial system. To establish a modern industrial system and implement *Pearl River Delta Development Plan*, the integration planning of the Pearl River Delta industrial layout pointed out the optimization of the layout, guiding the cross – administrative region industrial development, and promoting the optimization and efficient allocation of resource elements. In 2008, Guangdong accounted for only 11.9% of the total economy of China. Guangdong's GDP surpassed that of Singapore in 1998, surpassed that of Hong Kong in 2003, and exceeded that of Taiwan in 2007. According to purchasing power, if Guangdong is considered as a separate economy, its economy aggregate ranked 14th in the world in 2007. At the same time, the independent innovation capability has been increasing. The environment for innovation has been improving. High – tech industry has become an important force to promote Guangdong's economic growth.

3.2 Evolution and Current Features of Industrial Structure

3.2.1 Current Features

(1) Guangdong's big economic aggregate has a leading position in China. In 2013, the total assets of industrial companies above designated size in Guangdong amounted to 7965.527 billion Yuan, accounting for 9.1% of that in China, ranking third. The sales value was 10,685.368 billion Yuan, accounting for 10.5% of that of China, ranking third. The export delivery value was 3020.544 billion Yuan, accounting for 26% of that of the country, ranking first. Regarding employment, the number of those who work in industrial companies above designated size was 14.5581 million. Computer, communications and other electronic equipment manufacturing had the largest group of employees, accounting for 22.7% of the number of employees in industrial companies. Among traditional industries, the number of those who work in textile, clothing and fashion industry was relatively big, making up 6.9% of the total. Automobile manufacturing had 325,700 employers, making up 2.2%.

(2) The industrial structure has been optimized and economic benefit has been gradually increasing. The added value of Guangdong's high – tech manufacturing companies above designated size accounted

for 25.1% of that of all the companies above designated size, up 5.5% than 2008. That of advanced manufacturing made up 47.9% of that of industry above designated size. In particular, the proportion of equipment manufacturing was 39.6%, 2.8% higher than in 2008; private companies' proportion was 41.3%, 17.1% higher than 2008. As to the profitability of companies, the contribution rate of total assets of industrial companies above designated size was 14.53%, 0.21% higher; ratio of profits to cost was 6.46%, up 1.02% than 2008; total labor productivity was 182,303 Yuan per person, an increase of 64,363 Yuan per person.

(3) The Pearl River Delta is the main force of industrial economic development and regional economic development coordination need to be further enhanced. In 2013, the industrial added value of the Pearl River Delta accounted for 80.8% of that of all Guangdong's companies above designated size, and the ratio of employees was 83.0%. As to industrial investment, the proportion of industrial investment in the Pearl River Delta was 59.5%. The difference coefficient of regional industrial economy was 1.25, 0.09% lower than 2008, indicating that the two strategy—"double transfer" and the revitalization of eastern, western and northern Guangdong—have been effective to some extent.

(4) Guangdong's industry is highly concentrated, and leading companies have maintained strong momentum. In 2013, Guangdong's large and medium – sized enterprises developed well. The industrial added value of large enterprises accounted for 44.6% of that of the province's companies above designated size. Total profit accounted for 44.6%. The industrial added value of medium – sized companies accounted for 27.0%, and their total profit accounted for 24.9%. Six companies had a main business income of over 100 billion.

3.2.2 Analysis on its Evolution

(1) Industrial production has been expanding and economic benefit has been rising. In terms of the number of companies, due to the differences between various means of collecting statistics, the number of companies above designated size has witnessed little change. In 2013, companies above designated size in Guangdong accounted for 11.4% of that in China, down 0.9 % than 2008. In 2013, the total assets of industrial companies above designated size were 7,965.527 billion Yuan,

3.34 times that in 2004; the main business income was 10636.121 billion yuan, 3.67 times that in 2004; the total profit was 649.642 billion Yuan, 4.48 times that in 2004 ; income tax payable was 102.14 billion Yuan, 5.16 times that in 2004. Regarding the economic benefit indicators, the business situation has improved continuously. In 2013, the contribution rate of total assets increased by 4.01% than 4.01; the cost rate of profit was 1.18% higher than that in 2004; the total labor productivity was 144.2% higher than that in 2004; Product sales rate slightly fluctuated in 2013 to 97.43%, down by 0.36% than in 2004, up 0.3% than in 2008.

(2) Heavy industrialization has made significant progress and industrialization has gathered speed. As to the structure of light and heavy industry, the ratio of light and heavy industry in terms of assets, output value and employees, indicates that Guangdong's industrialization is gradually tilting to heavy industry. The Huffman proportion, which reflects the process of industrialization, rose from 0.8047 in 2008 to 1.4277 in 2013, indicating that industrialization was approaching the end of the third stage, and was close to the second stage.

(3) Industrial structure has been optimized and technological and capital contribution rate has increased. The relationship between Guangdong industrial economic growth and capital investment, technological progress and labor input is work out through the economic growth model of Solow. Capital elasticity $\alpha = 0.557$, labor output elasticity $\beta = 0.443$; capital investment is fixed assets at comparable price, labor input is the number of employees, and total industrial output is industrial added value at comparable price. After working out the contribution of different factors to the rate of industrial growth rate from 2000 to 2013, the results show that the contribution rate of technological progress in Guangdong's industrial economy has been increasing slowly. From 2000 to 2013, the contribution rate of technological progress to industrial growth was 49.1%, 1.7% higher than that from 2000 to 2004, and 0.1% lower than that from 2000 to 2008. Meanwhile, the contribution rate of capital has been increasing rapidly. It was 30.8% from 2000 to 2013, 10.1% and 5.4 % higher than that of from 2000 to 2004 and from 2000 to 2008 respectively. The contribution rate of labor was obviously declining, from 31.9% from 2000 to 2004 to 20.1% from 2000 to 2013.

3.3 Development Foundations of Manufacturing

Since the start of the reform and opening up in 1978, Guangdong Province has gradually developed from an agricultural province into a major manufacturing province. The rapid development of manufacturing has provided strong support for Guangdong. As a result, the total economy of Guangdong has ranked first among China's provinces for 27 consecutive years and Guangdong has become a major manufacturing center of China and the world. Guangdong's manufacturing development is mainly reflected in the following aspects.

(1) The scale advantages have been increasing. In 2015, the added value of manufacturing companies above designated size was about 420 billion US dollars, an increase of 6.8%, accounting for 37.5% of the province's GDP. If Guangdong is considered as a separate economy, the added value of Guangdong's manufacturing developed from the eleventh largest one in the world in 2008 into the fifth largest now.

(2) The manufacturing system is complete. Guangdong has almost all manufacturing categories listed in the United Nations industry classification system. Among the more than 400 major industrial products in China, the production of about 130 industrial products in Guangdong ranks among the top three in China's provinces and that of about 60 industrial products ranks first in China's provinces.

(3) The level of manufacturing has been rising. In the past 40 years, Guangdong's manufacturing development can be divided into four stages: the starting stage, from 1978 to 1990, was led by light industrial consumer goods industry, such as food and beverage, textile and garment and household appliances; the fast development stage, from 1991 to 1997, was led by electronic information, electrical machinery industry etc.; the rapid development stage, from 1998 to 2007, was led by petrochemical, steel and other heavy industries; the stage of transforming and development, from 2008 to the present, was led by new displays, software, Biological medicine, new materials and other emerging industries and advanced manufacturing. In 2015, the added value of Guangdong's advanced manufacturing (about 226 billion US dollars) and high – tech manufacturing (about 125.5 billion US dollars) accounted for 48.5% and 27.0% of the total added value of the province's companies

above designated size.

(4) The industry layout emphasizes collaboration and a division of labor. The total volume of manufacturing in nine cities in the Pearl River Delta accounts for more than 80% of that in Guangdong Province. The Pearl River Delta's role as the manufacturing center has become increasingly prominent with the Pearl River East Bank focusing on high – end electronic information industry and the Pearl River West Bank developing advanced equipment manufacturing. In 2015, the added value of the Pearl River East Bank's electronic information industry was about 90 billion US dollars and that of the Pearl River West Bank's equipment manufacturing was about 40 billion US dollars. At the same time, the supporting role of the industrial parks in the underdeveloped areas in eastern, western and northern Guangdong is increasingly important. In 2015, the added value of the 80 industrial parks in eastern, western and northern Guangdong was about 30 billion US dollars, up 20% year on year, making up one fourth of the total industry in these areas. These industrial parks have become important supporting force in the Pearl River Delta.

(5) There is fast – growing information infrastructure. In recent years, Guangdong has gathered speed in the construction of information infrastructure and vigorously promoted the integration of information technology and industrialization, facilitated the development of the Internet of things and cloud computing industry and the application of new technologies and models of the Internet in the economic and social fields. In 2015, the popularizing rate of the Internet reached 72.4% and the number of Internet users reached 77.68 million. The number of 4G base stations totaled 335,000, of which 147,000 were newly built, and there were about 48.96 million 4G users. The above indicators have a leading position in China. At present, the scale of the province's information consumption market has exceeded 150 billion US dollars. Shenzhen, Shantou, Zhuhai, Huizhou and Foshan have been listed in the country's first batch of information consumption pilot cities.

(6) The producer service industry has been growing. Guangdong's producer service industry has gradually developed, relying on the advantages of manufacturing, and a complete and efficient producer service system has been formed. Led by the rapid development of cloud computing, the Internet of things, mobile Internet and other emerging

services, Guangdong's industrial design, modern logistics and E – commerce have improved their quality and efficiency, thus providing strong support for the transformation and upgrading of Guangdong's industrial structure. In 2015, the added value of the province's producer service industry was about 295 billion US dollars, accounting for 26.5% of the province's GDP.

(7) Leading companies has been growing rapidly. By the end of 2015, in Guangdong there were 14 manufacturing companies that had an annual income of more than 10 billion US dollars as well as nearly 200 companies whose annual income exceeded 1 billion US dollars. Huawei, Gree, Midea and other leading companies are on the list of the world's top 500 corporations.

(8) It is highly marketized. Guangdong's total numbers of market bodies, private companies, foreign – funded companies, households of individual business, jobs created in manufacturing all rank first among the provinces of China.

(9) The innovative business environment has been increasingly optimized. The regional comprehensive innovation capacity of Guangdong ranks second among the provinces of China. The innovative business environment of Shenzhen and Guangzhou ranks first and second, respectively, among the cities of China,

3.4 Directions of Manufacturing's Future Development

In 2015, the Chinese government launched the "Made in China 2025" strategy. Guangdong, with biggest economy and manufacturing sector in China, responded by timely issuing *Recommendations on the Implementation of "Made in China 2025" in Guangdong* and *Development Plan of Intelligent Manufacturing in Guangdong (2015–2025). The Thirteenth Five – year Plan on Advanced Manufacturing in Guangdong* is currently in preparation and will soon be issued. Guangdong will focus on the implementation of the "Made in China 2025" strategy, give full play to its basic advantages in manufacturing and information technology, strengthen the industrial foundations, focus on integrated applications, adhere to the "high – end, intelligent, green and service – oriented" development path, with advanced equipment manufacturing being a breakthrough, intelligent manufacturing as the core and the main direction, through the integration of a new generation of information technology and manufacturing, thereby promoting the development of advanced manufacturing in Guangdong and leading the transformation and upgrading of Guangdong's manufacturing.

As to the direction of industrial development, Guangdong will focus on the development of four major industries and 18 sub – industries, such as a new generation of information technology, advanced equipment manufacturing, advanced materials manufacturing and bio – medicine manufacturing, in order to build an advanced manufacturing industry system in Guangdong.

In terms of the layout of industrial space, Guangdong will, along the traffic axis and the coastline, with the major industrial agglomeration area as the carrier, establish "three belts and two areas" including the Pearl River East Bank High – end Electronic Information Industry Belt, the Pearl River West Advanced Equipment Manufacturing Belt, the Coastal Advanced Materials Manufacturing Belt, the Pearl River Estuary Biomedical Industry Area and the Eastern, Western and Northern Guangdong Supporting Industry Area.

To facilitate the development of advanced manufacturing, Guangdong will focus on nine aspects, including accelerating the construction of a manufacturing innovation center and pilot areas for intelligent manufacturing, promoting service – oriented manufacturing and producer services, organizing manufacturing companies to jointly learn basic abilities, facilitating "Internet + " advanced manufacturing, building multinational manufacturing enterprises, advancing the standardization and quality improvement of equipment manufacturing and promoting the coordinated development of large, medium and small enterprises.

3.5 The Development of the Pearl River West Bank Industrial Belt

In 2015, the Chinese government launched the "Made in China 2025" strategy, thus transforming the task of building a major manufacturing country into a national strategy. Guangdong Province, as the largest economy in China and an important supporting force of China's manufacturing, took the initiative to take on the historical task of building a major manufacturing country. In January 2015, the Guangdong Provincial Government issued *The Layout and Planning of the Pearl River West Bank Advanced Equipment Manufacturing Belt (2015–2020)*, with a focus on Zhuhai, Foshan, Zhongshan, Jiangmen, Yangjiang, Zhaoqing, Shunde District and other cities on the Pearl River West Bank, to develop advanced equipment manufacturing that involves intelligent manufacturing equipment, ship and ocean engineering equipment, rail transportation equipment, energy saving equipment, aviation equipment, new energy equipment, automobiles, satellites and their application. The goal is, by 2020, building an advanced equipment manufacturing base, the output value of which is over 300 billion US dollars, creating an important engine for the transformation and upgrading of Guangdong's manufacturing and a new growth pole of Guangdong's economy.

A notable feature of the project is emphasizing collaborations and a division of labor among cities on the Pearl River West Bank. Zhuhai focuses on developing general aviation equipment manufacturing as well as ship and ocean engineering equipment manufacturing. Foshan focuses on developing automobiles manufacturing, intelligent manufacturing, energy saving and environmental protection equipment manufacturing. Zhongshan focuses on new energy equipment new energy equipment, satellite and application, satellites and their application industry. Jiangmen focuses on the development of rail transportation equipment manufacturing and auto parts manufacturing. Yangjiang focuses on the development of new energy equipment manufacturing and large – scale deepwater ocean engineering equipment manufacturing. Zhaoqing focuses on the development of auto parts manufacturing and energy saving equipment manufacturing. Shunde District focuses on the development of industrial robots manufacturing, CNC machining equipment manufacturing and other intelligent manufacturing. Favorable conditions for investing on the Pearl River West Bank are as follows.

(1) Huge market demand. At present, Guangdong is vigorously promoting the intelligent transformation, robot applications and equipment updates in traditional manufacturing companies. Ceramics, furniture, food and beverage, textile and clothing, and a large number of other traditional manufacturing enterprises will have a huge demand for industrial robots and related manufacturing equipment. The application density of robots in Guangdong Province (the number of industrial robots owned by 10,000 industry employees) is about 40 units, which is lower than the global level (66 units), far lower than that of Korea (478 units), Japan (314 units), Germany (292 units) and other developed countries. As is estimated by the International Robot Association, Guangdong's future market demand for robots will account for about one – third of that of China. In 2015, Guangdong has 41,000 units of industrial robots, an increase of 78.4%. In Guangdong's automobile industry, the ratio of component parts' output value to complete vehicles' was only 0.12: 1. Compared with the developed countries (1.7: 1) and China (0.42: 1), Guangdong's automobile industry has a huge room for growth.

(2) Favorable industrial policies. The Guangdong Provincial Government has allocated a budget of about US$4 billion to focus on supporting the construction of high – quality advanced equipment manufacturing projects in the Pearl River West Bank, the intensive development of the industrial agglomeration zone, the research, development and use of the first significant and advanced equipment and the construction of related research and development institutions. At the same time, the Pearl River West Advanced Equipment Manufacturing Fund, the total size of which is about 7.5 billion US dollars, is launched. Its focus is advanced equipment manufacturing projects, especially the manufacturing projects of machine tools.

(3) Adequate land supply. Compared with the Pearl River East Bank, the intensity of land development in the Pearl River West Bank is relatively low, with abundant construction land for industrial production. The Government of Guangdong Province has adopted special measures to first guarantee the land demand of the Pearl River West Advanced Equipment Manufacturing Belt.

(4) Strong growth momentum. In 2015, on the Pearl River West Bank, there were 179 newly – signed investment projects, each of which were worth over 15 million US dollars, 92 newly – constructed projects and 86 newly – launched production projects. The volume of investment on the Pearl River West Bank equipment manufacturing amounted to 18 billion US dollars, an increase of 56.8%. Emerson Electric Group and a number of other well – known US companies have settled on the Pearl River West Bank.

(5) Broad development consensus. In 2014, the Ministry of Industry and Information Technology of China and the People's Government of Guangdong Province signed the *Cooperation Agreement on the Development of the Pearl River West Bank Advanced Equipment Manufacturing Belt.* The Guangdong Provincial economic authorities and the cities on the Pearl River West Bank set up specialized agencies to promote the building of the industrial belt on the Pearl River West Bank. All levels of governments, business and communities have reached a broad consensus on the construction and development of the Pearl River West Bank.

(6) Rich human resources. In Guangdong, there are 141 colleges and universities, with its number of college students ranking second among China's provinces, 472 scientific research institutions and 511.000 R&D professionals, with its scale ranking first in China, as well as a large number of skilled workers.

(7) Efficient government services. In recent years, Guangdong Province has simplified the approval procedures of foreign investment and reduced over 90% of pre – approval items. To best facilitate business investment, Guangdong has comprehensively introduced online services hall so that companies can apply for investment projects on the Internet. In this way, Guangdong has realized the goal of "informing, accepting, dealing and supervising on the Internet".

(8) Convenient infrastructure. Guangdong has gathered speed in the construction of Central Pearl River Delta Intercity Track, Hong Kong – Zhuhai – Macao Bridge, Shenzhen – Zhongshan Bridge and other major infrastructure projects, connecting the Pearl River West Bank, Hong Kong and Macao together into a one – hour economic circle. At the same time, Guangdong Province has invested heavily in the three – year plan (2015–2017) of the construction of information infrastructure. By the end of 2017, fiber access capacity of Guangdong Province will reach 300Mbps, creating China's first broadband city group in the Pearl River Delta.

4. Economic and Trade Cooperation between Guangdong Province and Latin America

Latin America is one of the key emerging markets that Guangdong has been expanding. At present, Guangdong has gathered great momentum for import and export in Latin America and has made good progress in direct investment and economic cooperation.

4.1 General Situations of Economic and Trade Cooperation between Guangdong and Latin America

The economic and trade cooperation between Guangdong and Latin America is mainly through import and export. Over the past 10 years and beyond, the trade between Guangdong and Latin America has witnessed a rapid growth. In particular, since 2012, the growth rate has exceeded the overall growth rate of China – Latin America trade. In 2014, the total trade volume of Guangdong reached 39 billion US dollars, accounting for 14.8% of the total trade between China and Latin America and 3.6% of the province's total trade. Regarding trading products, major exports include mechanical and electrical products and high – tech products. In 2013, Guangdong's export volume of electromechanical products and high – tech products to Latin America were 18.75 billion US dollars and 9.18 billion US dollars respectively, accounting for 68.8% and 33.7% of Guangdong's total exports. Major imports are agricultural products. The import of fresh, dried fruits and nuts has witnessed rapid growth. Regarding forms of trade, general trade plays the leading role. In 2013, the import and export volume of general trade was 22.33 billion US dollars, accounting for 59.6% of the total trade volume of Guangdong; that of the processing trade was 11.52 billion US dollars, accounting for 30.7% of the total. As to trading bodies, foreign – invested companies have played a major role. In 2013, the trade between Guangdong's foreign – invested companies and Latin America totaled 17.68 billion US dollars, including 12.42 billion US dollars of exports and 5.26 billion US dollars of imports, accounting for 47.2% of the total trade volume of Guangdong and Latin America. However, since 2015, private companies have become increasingly important in Guangdong's trade with Latin America. The trade volume of private companies has made up more than half of the province's total trade with Latin America. As to trading regions, Guangdong has witnessed a growth of imports and exports in most Latin American countries. Its major trading partners include

Mexico, Brazil, Chile, Peru, Argentina and Panama.

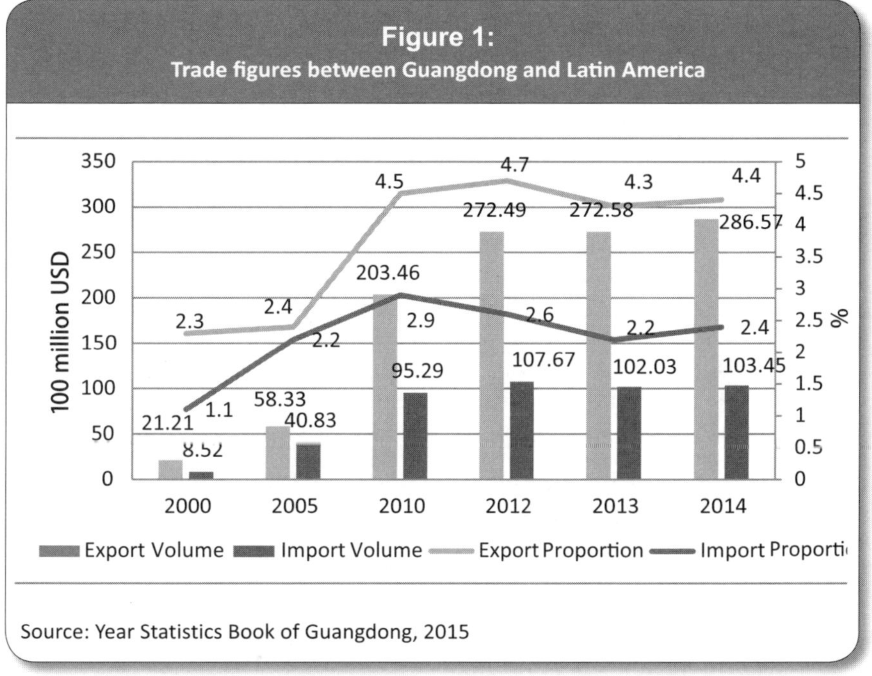

Figure 1:
Trade figures between Guangdong and Latin America

Source: Year Statistics Book of Guangdong, 2015

In the economic and trade cooperation between Guangdong and Latin America, investment and economic cooperation has been increasing. In terms of the utilization of foreign investment, in 2013, Guangdong approved five FDI projects from South America, with 26.85 million US dollars of contractual foreign investment. Regarding the regions for foreign investment and cooperation, in 2013, Guangdong's direct investment in Latin American countries totaled 470 million US dollars. The main destinations of Guangdong's direct investment in Latin America include the British Virgin Islands, Brazil, the Cayman Islands, Mexico, Peru and Colombia. Major companies that have been investing in Latin America are Huawei, ZTE, Zhuhai Gree and Midea. At present, the sources and destinations of the bilateral investment and trade are mainly concentrated in the Pearl River Delta region and the relatively backward areas of northern Guangdong are not yet covered.

4.2 The Economic and Trade Interests of Guangdong Province in Latin America

China has become the second largest trading partner and the third largest source of investment of Latin America. Latin America has become the largest overseas market for Chinese products and capital for nearly a decade. Similarly, in Guangdong's foreign trade, Latin America also plays an increasingly important role. Research shows that all the respondents hope to expand economic and trade cooperation and show much less interest in other forms of cooperation. They believe that, against the backdrop of economic slowdown in China and Latin America, further strengthening the China – Latin America economic and trade cooperation is beneficial for China to achieve the scale effect of superior production capacity and ease the economic imbalance. It can also help Latin America improve its infrastructure and thus change the single economic structure. Therefore it is not only an effective means to achieve win – win results, but also the cornerstone of the overall cooperation between China and Latin America.

As to the driving force of cooperation, the demand in trade cooperation is declining while the demand for investment cooperation is rising. China – Latin America economic and trade cooperation has been focusing on trade. Investment and economic cooperation has been developing in parallel. Between 2000 and 2012, China – Latin America trade remained at an average annual growth rate of over 30%, while investment growth was relatively slow; but since 2012, trade and investment growth has switched positions, and China's investment in Latin America has gathered speed. Research shows that over the past decade or so, there had been a significant increase in researched places' investment in Latin America, with the growth rate of their proportion in the total trade volume ranging from 3–9%. But recently, the relative size of the trade with Latin America has been stable or even decreasing minimally. This shows that, through the complementary trade, Chinese companies have completed or initially completed their "spontaneous" expansion of the Latin American market, and that some companies have begun to seek a way to optimize the allocation of resources, "consciously" explore the potential of Latin America through investment and maximize the income in the Latin American market.

In terms of cooperation motives, markets and resources are the main drivers. Research shows that the China – Latin America trade structure is highly concentrated. In researched regions, major imports include iron ore, metal products, agricultural and sideline products, paper pulp and integrated circuits. At the same time, Latin America has become one of the scaled markets of the goods manufactured by China. Major exports include machinery, electronic products, clothing, textiles, chemicals and hardware tools. The trade products of the researched regions are well – suited to the local industrial structure. So the resources and markets of Latin America and that of researched regions are generally complementary. In terms of investment, companies in researched regions have a clear tendency in choosing investment destinations. Companies manufacturing electronic appliances and other consumer products are market – oriented and tend to choose scaled markets to make investment, such as Brazil, Argentina and Mexico. Companies manufacturing smelting petrochemical and other resource – based products are resource – oriented and tend to choose resources origins, such as Peru, Brazil, Chile, Venezuela and Bolivia.

To sum up, in the period of the new normal of the Chinese economy, Latin America will become China's supplier of resources, energy and intermediate products, a recipient of advantage products and production capacity, an implementer of innovative technology and standards as well as an important partner in overseas economic strategies. Therefore, Latin America is related to China's key economic interests. China – Latin America cooperation will help promote the integration of each other's industrial chain, form a new value chain, diversify the trade structure, and facilitate the operation of three major engines—trade, investment and financial cooperation—so as to achieve the comprehensive upgrading of in China – Latin America economic and trade cooperation.

5. Difficulties and Challenges in Economic and Trade Cooperation between Guangdong Province and Latin America

At present, China – Latin America economic and trade cooperation is at the stage of restructuring, facing both domestic and foreign pressure.

On the one hand, the goals of economic and trade cooperation, which has been the engine of China – Latin America relations, is becoming more and more diversified. To upgrade the cooperation structure and transform the driving force, it is necessary to clear the institutional bottlenecks in the process of shifting from "spontaneous" cooperation to "conscious" cooperation. On the other hand, the external environment hinders the expansion of China – Latin America cooperation. As a sample area, Guangdong is also facing difficulties in further expanding its economic and trade cooperation with Latin America. Research shows that the cooperation between Guangdong and Latin America faces a variety of risks in the short term, and it is subject to a series of institutional constraints.

First, some risks are brought by cyclical factors in Latin America. Latin American countries generally lack economic independence and are vulnerable to the global economic cycle, because Latin America's overall level of industrialization is not high, the proportion of the first and tertiary industries are both relatively high and major exports are primary commodity. Influenced by the dual intertwined factors of the economic cycle and the financial cycle, Latin American countries' exchange rate, inflation and wage growth take turns to fluctuate. Research shows that, since 2013, Latin America's economic slowdown, intensified inflation and Brazil, Argentina, Venezuela and other major economic and trade partners' intensified devaluation have posed negative influences on the economic interests of Chinese companies and China's confidence in export and investment.

Second, some risks are brought by Latin American policies. Latin American labor and environmental legislation and standards are relatively advanced. Because of the historical debt crisis, foreign exchange control is strict. Research shows that the current policies mainly cause three types of potential risks on Chinese companies. One is the risks of profit repatriation. Argentina and other countries implement foreign exchange control, so Chinese companies often complain that it is difficult to repatriate profits. Two is labor risks. The big lack of skilled labor and the high standards of labor protection in Latin America make a "weak government and strong trade unions". The government's decision – making is manipulated by the interest groups. Many researched companies said that they found it difficult to hire labor or those they once encountered strikes. Three is the risks of environmental conflicts. The high legislation and standards of the environment, strong non – governmental environmental organizations, ecological and environmental conflicts of Indian indigenous peoples add uncertainty to introducing foreign investment. As a result, many projects of the researched companies failed eventually.

Third, there are problems in the business environment in Latin America. Latin America's overall business environment is subject to institutional constraints. Researched companies mainly have five types of problems. One is the high local production costs, which cover labor, logistics, tax and other aspects of explicit or implicit costs. Two is that the complex procedures of establishing new companies take a long time in most Latin American countries. Three is the poor social security situation. Violent crime rate and murder rate there more than double that in other regions. Four is the timeliness of bilateral cooperation is greatly compromised because applying for a visa takes a long time and many countries require the application of a reverse visa. Five is the arbitrary policy formulation and implementation to some extent, with the introduction of Argentina's regulations on import quota being a typical example; adding uncertainty to Chinese companies' local trade and investment.

Fourth, there exist policy and institutional constraints on "going global". Some of the current local policies only give inadequate support to Chinese companies' operation and some even impose constraints. One is financial constraints. Companies in the "going global" process are constrained by the existing financial system, suffering from high financing costs and severe difficulties. Therefore financial policies need to be further improved and innovated. Two is staff constraints. Cooperation and exchange are hindered by the long approval process and limited time of business visits to Latin America. Three is the constraints of supporting policies. The current supporting policies and measures on "going global" is not advanced enough to deal with the risks brought about by the overall China – Latin America cooperation strategies.

Fifth, the absence of trading bodies. The export capacity of many resource – rich countries is severely restricted by Latin America's poor infrastructure. So Latin America expects China to invest in the construction of roads and port facilities. This is difficult to achieve in the traditional mode that features companies being trading bodies. Latin American governments cannot pay a large amount of money for construction, so they have to sign agreements similar to export agreements of agricultural products and resource products. This problem is common in Latin America. Having gone through the stage of companies' "spontaneous" cooperation, China – Latin America economic and trade cooperation is facing the increasingly severe absence of potential trading bodies.

Sixth, Chinese companies lack overseas business management capacities. Research shows that their lack of overseas management capacities is reflected mainly in three aspects. One is that entrepreneurs need to improve their personal qualities and abilities in cross – cultural understanding and learning. Two is the internal governance structure within companies needs to be optimized. Three is the construction of external social network needs to be strengthened.

Seventh, the problem of vicious competition among companies is acute. Chinese companies' fierce competition in Latin America can be rated as vicious competition. Therefore, Chinese companies' profits in the Latin American market are further diluted. An important part of Guangdong's foreign trade is OEM production. Against the backdrop of a completely competitive market, giving low quotations for competition is detrimental to Guangdong and even China. In this regard, companies researched hope that the government can introduce some guiding measures and programs to reduce vicious competition's damage to the industry.

6. Primary Conclusions and Policy Recommendations

Regarding the economic structure of Guangdong province and Latin America, the two economies are highly complementary. The research on Guangdong Province shows that stable and predictable economic and trade cooperation between China and Latin America is in line with the common interests of both sides and can become the focus of the overall cooperation. China should lead the top – level design of the cooperation framework, reduce the institutional constraints and risks of the current cooperation and promote positive expansion of bilateral economic and trade cooperation, thereby creating favorable conditions for full cooperation. In order to eliminate the unfavorable factors in China – Latin America cooperation, recommendations are as follows:

First, build an overall cooperation platform based on companies. Due to the imbalance between China and Latin America in terms of visions and capacity, China should lead the top – level design of the cooperation and build the mechanism and framework for overall cooperation, thereby creating favorable conditions for full cooperation in the future. Therefore, it is important for the government to coordinate and set up the overall cooperation platform for companies, negotiate and formulate the strategy for the development of China – Latin America cooperation, and expand the scope of the bilateral free trade agreement. This is not only the fundamental guarantee for better cooperation with Latin America in the future, but also an important step to deepen future cooperation. This platform can ease the problem of "lack of potential trading body" in China – Latin America cooperation and deal with Latin American governments' limited governance capacity. It can also integrates infrastructure construction, import and export and financial services, and help to transform the great deal of potential cooperation into reality.

In detail, we can facilitate Chinese companies' business in Latin America from the following aspects: we can simplify the procedures of overseas M&A and lower the fee level, so as to reduce the costs and improve the efficiency of M&A; we can formulate policies to encourage Chinese law firms to expand overseas business or to cooperate with overseas firms in order to provide advices and legal help to Chinese companies; we can promote the RMB settlement business and facilitate overseas investment by lowering lending rates and other means; we can open new sea routes to Latin America through the Pacific Ocean and improve the efficiency of China – Latin America economic and trade cooperation and exchange.

Second, improve the platform for companies' comprehensive information exchange and services. A diversified, professional and comprehensive information service platform for companies is an important guarantee of further strengthening the economic and trade cooperation between China and Latin America. Recently, the Chinese Ministry of Commerce launched a public platform for "going global"—http://fec.mofcom.gov.cn/—to help companies know basic information and risks of investment destinations. Besides, it is necessary to consider the needs of Chinese companies, organize "going global" companies to share experiences and lessons, summarize the needs of different companies, existing typical problems and political problems, and report them to the governments of China and Latin American countries. This cooperation can be realized through many ways, including cooperation with domestic and foreign research institutions, Latin American embassies and all types of companies, with the aim of building a multi – participant, professional and comprehensive platform for information exchange service.

Third, build a mechanism to avoid Latin American exchange rate risk. In the face of many Latin American countries' excessive currency volatility and the limited coverage of China – Latin America currency swap agreement, integrating innovative financial services has become the top primary in order to avoid financial risks. China should strive to promote Chinese banks' cooperation with insurance companies and bonding companies so as to attract Latin American banks and other financial services institutions to enter this field. This can not only help bypass the dollar settlement, avoid Latin American countries' foreign exchange control to some extent, but also contribute to the conclusion of the currency swap agreement, which can serve for Chinese companies' import and export. In addition, this can help shorten the settlement cycle and the approval time of cooperation projects in Latin America (Dollar settlement projects in Latin America is subject to approval by their congress, so the procedures take a long time.), and further promote the establishment of offshore market and clearing market.

Fourth, enhance the administrative efficiency of the mechanism. Regarding administrative efficiency, the Government should shorten the procedures, after careful consideration of the needs of companies in terms of customs clearance and tax refund. Free trade areas can be used as pilot areas, where import and export procedures should be renewed and approval items should be reduced in order to achieve policy simplification and to upgrade old rules and regulations. Besides, the government should also establish coordination and right protection mechanisms to support companies as well as guide companies to adopt more appropriate strategies in different cycles.

In addition, China's think tanks, the Institute of Latin American Studies of the CASS in particular, should better identify the right tasks, seize the opportunity of the comprehensive upgrading of China – Latin America cooperation, study Latin America from the perspective of China and continuously adjust the directions and focuses of researches, so as to not only provide professional policy recommendations to the government, but also give advice, counseling and warnings on practical questions raised by companies.

Yue Yunxia is a full professor in the ILAS, CASS. She's now the Associate Director of the Department of Economics in ILAS of CASS, where she specializes on the China – Latin American economic relations, as well as the international economics, international trade, and FDI. Her recent publications include "On Colombia's Openness in Service Trade and Its Inspiration to FTA with China – An Comparison on Four FTAs", "Trade Effect of China – Chilean FTA: A Post Analysis with Gravity Model", "Latin American Trade Frictions against China", "Potential and Environment of China – Latin America Economic Cooperation", "Game in China – Latin America Trade" "Outlook of China – Mexico Trade", "Invest in Latin America and the Caribbean VS. China's Energy Security' and "Economic and Social Effects of the Outward – oriented Development Model in Latin America".

Zhang Yong, male, is the associate research fellow in the Institute of Latin American Studies (ILAS), Chinese Academy of Social Sciences (CASS). He gained his MA in management and Ph.D. in economics from Graduate School of CASS (GSCASS) in 2003 and 2008 respectively. He joined ILAS in 2003 and since then he has devoted himself to academic studies about Latin American economy and development. His research fields include economic development, labor mobility and employment, and international trade and investment. Since 2008 he has paid more attention to Sino – Latin American economic relations in the context of the international financial crisis, food crisis and agriculture in Latin America, and transformation of economic growth model in Latin America and the Caribbean (LAC) countries.

Xie Wenze, Ph.D. in World Economy, Investigator, Professor of the Institute of Latin American Studies (ILAS) Chinese Academy of Social Sciences (CASS). Research interests concern the Cities and National Development, Urban Development, Rural Development, Industrialization, Public policies for Sustainable Development.

Introduction of Silk Road Academy:

Silk Road Academy ("SRA"): The Chinese Academy of Social Sciences ("CASS") and the China Association for the Promotion of Development Financing ("CAPDF") work together to implement the requirements of the China-Belarus joint declaration made during President Xi Jinping's visit to Belarus, and establish the Silk Road Academy ("SRA"). With its working framework covering all the countries and regions along the "Belt and Road", SRA aims to provide intellectual and talent support to the "Belt and Road" construction, and promote common development of these regions. SRA, by fully mobilizing research forces and think tank resources and liaising with government departments and businesses, will carry out training for countries along the "Belt and Road", including introducing the policies, ideas and measures in relation to the "Belt and Road" construction, promoting interconnection, interworking and practical cooperation under the "Belt and Road" framework, and communicating China's development experience.

Introduction of CSSP:

Established in June, 1978, China Social Sciences Press is sponsored by Chinese Academy of Social Sciences. CSSP is a national level publishing house focusing on academic publications mainly in the field of humanities and social sciences. In 1993, CSSP won the honorary title of "national outstanding press" granted by Propaganda Department of CPC and General Administration of Press and Publication.

Since its establishment, with the strategic idea of combinations of social and economic benefits, quantity and quality improvement, individual and company development, CSSP has been persisting in publishing academic and professional works of philosophy and social sciences. With an attitude of professionalization, specialization, digitalization, internationalization and popularization, CSSP has gained its goals of profit increase, brand promotion, market expansion and industry innovation.

Large numbers of excellent monographs and book series have been published by CSSP since its establishment. During the process, it united and gathered most first-level scholars and authors as well as exchanged copyright with scores of countries and areas in the world. Till now, CSSP has published almost 20,000 titles and achieved the annual goal of more than 1,000 titles that are great academic research works, culture works and most valuable research fruits from experts and scholars of CASS. Among the publications, hundreds of these won various national book prizes and rewards.

In order to better promote the Belt and Road Initiative put forward by China, the China Social Sciences Press (CSSP) selected eight books from the National Think Tank Report, the brand of the CSSP Think Tank, and have jointly launched their English version with the Silk Road Academy. These books are highly consistent with the topics of the Belt and Road Forum for International Cooperation to be held May 14-15, 2017.